AFTER THE ACADEMY:
Memories of Teaching and Learning in the Land of Lincoln

Edited by
Larry LaFond, William Retzlaff
and Aldemaro Romero

*For Wayne,
with my best wishes*
Al Romere

After the Academy:

Memories of Teaching and Learning in the Land of Lincoln

Copyright © 2012 Board of Trustees of Southern Illinois University
Governing Southern Illinois University Edwardsville

All rights reserved
Manufactured in the U.S.A.

ISBN-10: 0-9798499-2-6
ISBN-13: 978-0-9798499-2-3

Cover and interior design by Vickie Swisher, Studio 20\20

The paper used in this publication meets the minimum requirements of the American National Standard of Permanence of Paper for Printed Library Materials Z39.48-1984

Library of Congress Cataloging-in-Publication Data

After the academy : memories of teaching and learning in the land of Lincoln /
Edited by Larry LaFond, William Retzlaff, and Aldemaro Romero.
   pages cm
   Includes index.
   ISBN 978-0-9798499-2-3 (softcopy : alk. paper) — ISBN 978-0-9798499-3-0 (ebook)
   1. Southern Illinois University Edwardsville—Faculty—Anecdotes.
I. LaFond, Larry, 1959- II. Retzlaff, William, 1959- III. Romero Díaz, Aldemaro 1951-
LD5101.S364A385 2012
378.773'86—dc23
2012003544

Printed in the U.S.A.

Contents

Foreword: Vignettes from the Past__**vii**
RALPH W. AXTELL & WILLIAM A. RETZLAFF

The Journey__**1**
WILLIAM GRIVNA

The Simultaneous Pursuit of Passions and Paychecks—
It Can Be Done!__**13**
SHEILA VOSS

Reflections__**21**
JACK G. SHAHEEN

Ruth Slenczynska, The Pianist Who Took Her Future in Her Hands__**33**
ALDEMARO ROMERO

SIUE in the 1970s: Building a University and Starting a Career__**47**
JOE MUNSHAW

Accidental Achievement__**59**
MARIAN SMITH

Leadership and Culture:
Overcoming Challenges and Building a Future__**73**
DAVID SILL

Becoming an Artist Educator: The Journey at SIUE__**91**
JOSEPH A. WEBER

S-I-U-E… & Me…__**105**
EUGENE B. REDMOND

More Than Serendipity?__**115**
ERNEST L. SCHUSKY

John D. Kendall Dies at 93; Leader in Music Training__**123**
MARGALIT FOX

Journey to Success__**133**
RANCE THOMAS

The Long and Winding Road__**145**
GONZALO JOSE JOVE CUSICANQUI

Unique Opportunities in Higher Education:
Some Thoughts from a Retired Sociology Professor__**159**
JOHN E. FARLEY

In Academia as Well, What's Past is Prologue__**167**
ALDEMARO ROMERO

About the Authors__**171**

Index__**181**

VIGNETTES
from the Past

by RALPH W. AXTELL
(*With commentary by* WILLIAM RETZLAFF)

In 2010, a remarkable collection of essays chronicling the academic journeys of faculty from the College of Arts and Sciences of Southern Illinois University Edwardsville (SIUE) were published in *Adventures in the Academy: Professors in the Land of Lincoln and Beyond* (ed. by Larry LaFond, Charles Berger, and Aldemaro Romero). This second volume, *After the Academy: Memories of Teaching and Learning in the Land of Lincoln,* gives the reader a broader look at the academy through a focus on the experiences and journeys of distinguished alumni and emeritus faculty from SIUE. I take great pleasure in introducing this volume, in no small part because I have been a part of SIUE as a faculty member for 52 years, nearly its entire history. My introduction—my "memories of teaching"—take the form of a series of vignettes from the past. As will be chronicled, SIUE had a fairly tumultuous beginning. During the period of the University's history, between 1957 and 1960, there was some question whether the new university would even become a part of the SIU system. If it had not, one might wonder what a completely separate new institution might have been like today. Would we have a medical school in Springfield, a dental school in Alton, a College of Arts and Sciences, and Schools of Business, Education, Engineering, Nursing, and Pharmacy here in Edwardsville? These are questions that will never be answered, because circumstances and people have led us to where we are today. While I have been at SIUE, there have been six administrations and top administrators, Delyte Morris, John Rendleman, Buzz Shaw, Earl Lazerson, David Werner, and our present Chancellor, Vaughn Vandegrift. With Chancellor Vandegrift's retirement next year, we now anticipate there will be a new SIUE Chancellor in July 2012. My vignettes relate to some of these earlier times, times when rapid expansion in uncharted areas was occurring. Other chapters in this volume will tell the stories of teaching and learning that occurred at SIUE in a variety of ways: through personal recollections, interviews, creative work, poetry, even posthumously through a touching reprinted article remembering an emeritus faculty member who recently passed away. We hope you enjoy this exploration of how people's journeys led them to SIUE, what they experienced while there, and what they have taken with them from the experience.

Now, on to my recollections:

Helicopter Ride:

When I first came to SIU in the fall of 1960, we had two campuses, one at the old Shurtleff College in Alton, and the other at the old high school building in East Saint Louis. There were five biology faculty at the time, Harold Broadbooks, Donal Myer, and I at Alton, and Joseph Davis and Harold Pfeifer at East St. Louis. The future campus in Edwardsville was still large homesteads, some farms with cultivated land, and others with considerable forest cover. There was even a horse track on one of the properties (more details about this property later in this section). President Delyte Morris and his staff were

Faculty prepare to view the future campus by helicopter.
PHOTOGRAPH COURTESY OF PHOTOGRAPHIC SERVICES COLLECTION, UNIVERSITY ARCHIVES, LOVEJOY LIBRARY.

developing plans for the new campus and, presumably, had already activated eminent domain proceedings. In order to show off the new campus site, faculty from both teaching centers were invited out one Sunday afternoon to observe the future campus area in a helicopter provided by the University. Will Shaw from the Physics Faculty (we didn't have departments then) and Dale Blount from the Technical and Adult Education Program took their helicopter ride just before me, and as they moved over the future central campus area, they noticed a man below carrying a shotgun (I learned only recently it was Leopold A. Freund). A few seconds later a report was heard from below, and those in the helicopter realized that the person below was firing at them. They quickly returned to the landing site, and exited the machine to examine it for damage. Finding only minor damage to the rotor blades and none to the subsurface of the body, the pilot decided to continue his observation flights. Being the next in line, a colleague (whose name I do not remember) and I climbed into the machine and took off in a direction away from the Freund Farm. We gained altitude so I could see the entire future campus well. I do not remember who the next riders were after we returned to the landing site. Mr. Blount and Dr. Shaw later filed a complaint against Mr. Freund, but in 1961 they asked the state's attorney to drop the charges. On 16 January 1961, the University announced its purchase of the 132-acre Freund Farm for $155,000. That farm, with its official-sized horse race track, now forms part of the Stratton Quadrangle.

(I thank Steve Kerber, the SIUE Library Archivist, for his help in the preparation of this vignette.)

Naming SIUE:

Several years after arriving at the "Alton Residence Center" (the old Shurtleff College campus, where the School of Dental Medicine is now located), I developed a new field course in herpetology (The study of amphibians [salamanders, frogs and toads] and reptiles [turtles, snakes, lizards, and crocodilians]). At that time we had no preserved collection with which to work, so I decided to start one (which I still maintain in my lab today). This was appropriate then because no state laws had yet been passed restricting collection of living organisms for use in teaching and research at state institutions. If such a collection is to be useful, however, every specimen collected must be tagged in some way, identifying the collection location and date, given an identifying number, and then catalogued. The collection itself must also be identified so it can be differentiated from any other similar collection in the world. This requires an acronym such as FMNH (for Field Museum of Natural History, in Chicago) on the tag. Since I knew we would eventually be moving to the new campus in Edwardsville, I used the acronym **SIUE** on our tags, along with an individual number for each specimen placed in the collection. As far as I know, this was the first time these four letters had ever appeared in this context. Later, when the faculty was asked to suggest possible names for the new university, I suggested SIUE. The rest is history. I was never officially notified of this name adoption, however. Much later (about 2005), the bold E was first introduced in black, and then a little later it was changed to red. Last year, I asked Chancellor

Vandegrift who had come up with the bold red e, and he replied that he had done it to draw attention to this university. I certainly would agree with him that it has.[1]

While much of the above (1957 to early 1960) was going on, Dr. Harold W. See, who had recently been named Vice President of what was then called the Southwestern Illinois Campus (which included both the Alton and East St. Louis Residence Centers), apparently had independently decided that this institution should be named Southwestern Illinois University and, therefore, would not be a part of Southern Illinois University. What had happened next was unknown to me, but when I arrived in the fall of 1960, Dr. See was no longer in evidence, and I never heard his name uttered by any of those in charge at the time.

Our Edwardsville Earthquake:

My experience with earthquakes dates back to 1946/1948 when I was with the U.S. Army occupation forces in Japan. Several quakes occurred while I was there, but none that were over 5.0 on the Richter scale. One of the things I remember quite well, however, was the noise. I could hear the quake coming! It sounded like a very low amplitude roar or rumble.

I didn't realize it at the time, but at 11:02 a.m. on November 9, 1968, I heard that sound again, and it wasn't in Japan this time, but in Edwardsville, Illinois. I was walking eastward down the north hallway of the first floor of the lab wing in the Science Building, and noted that the floor in front of me was bending up and down like a bath towel being shaken by a person. I quickly ran out the east end of the building and looked westward at the new Science Building office wing then under construction. The elongate, square, vertical cement

---

[1] [Editor's Note: Designations for SIUe in this volume will appear in different forms (e.g., SIU, SIU-E, SIU at Edwardsville, SIUE, SIUe). These variant forms were used at differing times in the history of the University, and the choices made here attempt to reflect the historical usage at the time of events discussed].

piers (no floors were present yet) of the new addition were swaying about 15 degrees back and forth! I did not go back into the building, and frankly can't remember what I did do.

Later, I learned that this was a 5.4 magnitude quake, whose epicenter was reportedly in the Wabash Valley seismic zone at 37°56'59"N – 88°28'48"W, near the town of Broughton in southern Hamilton Co., IL. The quake was felt in 23 states over an area of 580,000 square miles. No casualties were reported, but the event caused considerable structural damage to buildings. The only damage I noticed to the Science Building was one of the huge glass windows on the east side of the auditorium was cracked. The new Science Building, now under construction, has been designed to meet a more recent seismic code.

When studied later, this quake revealed a new and previously unknown east-west fault, now called the Cottage Grove Fault. This 16 mile deep fault runs along an ancient, buried Precambrian terrain boundary. It was believed active mainly in late Pennsylvanian and early Permian time, around 300 million years ago![2]

Early Field trips to the Southwest:

From 1971 to 1986, I offered summer field courses to various areas in the southwestern U.S. Although these courses had biology course numbers, they weren't restricted to biological subjects. We studied geology, geomorphology, geography, and climatology as we moved from place to place. We took similar routes on most of these trips. Leaving from Edwardsville, we usually traveled west to Kansas City and then to Lawrence, Kansas to visit the small, but excellent Museum of Natural History at the University of Kansas. In late June of 1972, I went on one of these field course trips, with three graduate

---

[2] *GSA Bulletin;* November 2004; v. 116; no. 11-12; p. 1465-1484; DOI: 10.1130/B25413.1 © 2004 Geological Society of America; also, W. John Nelson and Donald K. Lumm's 1987 *Structural Geology of Southeastern Illinois and Vicinity.* Department of Energy and Natural Resources, Illinois State Geological Survey, Circular 538.

students, Max Gricevich (who studied vascular plants), Walter Boyce (who studied insects), and Tim Weyenberg (who studied mammals). We traveled in two vehicles, both VW's, with Boyce and I in my microbus, and Gricevich, and Weyenberg in Max's hatchback. Moving west, we crossed the Oklahoma border near Elkhart, Kansas. We filled up with gas in Boise City, Oklahoma for $3.74 (number of gallons not remembered), but gas at that time was selling for about $0.30 a gallon! Continuing along the upper Cimarron River, we moved into Colorado near Branson, then northwest to Walsenburg, and west along U.S. 160 to our June 21 camp, 6 miles east of South Fork, Colorado. We did not stay in designated camping sites or in motels, but usually found a side road where we could exit far from the main highway. The students slept on cots under the stars and I slept in my microbus. After leaving western Kansas, we made numerous stops to investigate vegetation types, any wildlife we encountered, geology, and geomorphology. By 29 June we had reached Durango, Colorado, after which we traveled to the Four Corners region, the only place in the U. S. where you can stand in four states at the same time. Here we saw western Prairie Dogs *(Cynomys gunnisoni)* for the first time. We then moved back into Colorado, and took a cold swim in the San Juan River, where we saw several lizards climbing on the red sandstone outcroppings on the banks. We stopped for a short time to investigate Shiprock, an imposing, extinct volcanic neck now stripped of most of its surrounding sediments. We moved next into northeastern Arizona, and then across the Utah border through Monument Valley to Mexican Hat on the San Juan River. Then we turned around, and made our way back to Kayenta, Arizona, from there we headed southwest on U.S. 164 & 89 into the Painted Desert and on to Cameron, Arizona. On 30 June, we camped just above Muleshoe Bend near the east entrance to Grand Canyon National Park. Here we found the lizards I was looking for, so we returned to Cameron the next day and headed north toward Page, Arizona on U.S. 89. Just outside Page, the coil on my VW van blew up, so we went into Page and bought a new one. Page housed many of the construction workers for the new Glen

Ralph Axtell in his office.
PHOTOGRAPH BY ZHI-QING LIN.

Canyon Dam over the Colorado River. We remained in the Page area until 2 July, because that area was inhabited by several very interesting lizards (later in my career one of the lizards I studied on this trip was named after me). From the Page area we crossed into Utah, had lunch in Kanab, and took U.S. 89 north to Mt. Carmel, where we turned west on Utah 15 toward Zion National Park. Zion is best known for its huge scarps and monoliths of compressed and solidified eolian sand dunes (Navajo Sandstone) from the Early Jurassic Period, about 160 million years ago. Zion is located on the extreme western edge of the Colorado Plateau Province, a huge uplifted region that stretches all the way from western Utah to central New Mexico. More specifically, the park lies at the southern end of the Markagunt Plateau of the so called High Plateaus Section of the Colorado Plateau. We crossed the Virgin River Bridge near Hurricane and proceeded on to St. George, Utah. On 3 July we made camp in the Beaver Dam Mountains of extreme southwestern Utah, where we encountered a four and one-half foot long Great Basin Rattlesnake *(Crotalus viridus)* on the side of the same hill where we camped. This was the largest rattler seen on our trip. Moving southwestward into Nevada, we took Nevada 12 along the west side of Lake Mead, crossed Boulder Dam, and then reentered Arizona on U.S. 93. From 93 we turned off on the Dolan Springs road, and drove to Antelope Springs to camp (on July 4th) near a dry cattle tank. I was especially interested in this area because I had found two different collared lizard species hybridizing here several years earlier. We remained in this area until 5 July, and then moved south to Kingman, and later to Wikieup, Arizona. Southeast of Wikieup we visited the new Burrow Creek Campground and took a refreshing swim, our first bath in about eight days! Next, we moved off U. S. 93 to AZ 97 and then on AZ 96 to Bagdad where we camped at an overlook north of town (6 July). We spent much of the morning working the extensive basalt fields near Bagdad, and then headed southeast to Wickenburg, Avondale, and Buckeye during the afternoon heat (ca 110° F). On 7 July, we camped at a small lake near Painted Rock Dam on the Gila River. The next morning we spotted an adult male Great Basin Collared Lizard *(Crotaphytus bicinctores)* sitting on a dark cinder block near camp. I considered this an important and exciting find. The next day we drove into Tempe, Arizona to visit a friend and colleague and examine specimens at the Arizona State University there. We remained in Tempe until 10 July, and then headed north to Flagstaff, then Winslow (standing on the corner!), and Holbrook, Arizona. On 11 July, we arrived in Albuquerque where we visited the University of New Mexico again to examine specimens in their collections. Moving along rapidly, we soon passed through Santa Rosa and Tucumcari, and crossed into the Texas panhandle east of Nara Visa, New Mexico. We passed through Dalhart, crossed the Oklahoma panhandle, and made our last camp (12 July) near Cullison, Kansas. The next day we passed through Hutchinson, KS and reaching Lawrence again, stayed at Bill Duellman's place on 13 July. We arrived home the same day. We had traveled 4,426 miles in 17 days! At the time of the trip, these educational experiences were termed "field schools" or "summer camps" and many curricula had these practical experiences as part of the requirements. In modern terminology, these "field schools" or "summer camps" would be billed as "experiential learning". I note that faculty still continues to create experiences in their classroom and laboratories for students like those of the past and that SIUE is recognized nationally for it senior assignment program—something that was started by early faculty and staff.

Climbing Popo, the second highest mountain in Mexico:

In 1950, my colleagues, Jim Dixon and Linton Robertson, and I had the opportunity to climb the Mexican stratovolcano called Popocatepétl (which in Nahuatl, the Aztec language, means "smoking mountain"). This 17,880 foot (5450 m) peak is situated about 43 miles southeast of Mexico City on the boundary between the Mexican Federal District (Distrito Federal) and the state of Puebla. Popo, as it is known to locals, is considered an active volcano, because it comes to life occasionally, and at those times spews forth considerable steam and ash. At the time of our climb, we noted only a slight cloud coming from the crater, so we considered it safe for climbing. An unpaved ash road up the west side of the mountain lead to the Paso de Cortés, a ca12,370 foot saddle between "The Sleeping Lady" Iztaccihuatl (Nahuatl for "white lady") to the north, and Popo to the south. In this pass we set up our tents below the tree line, hoping to stay for several days to acclimate to the high elevation. What we had not anticipated, however, was that we found it difficult, if not impossible to sleep at this elevation! After two days without much rest, we decided to go ahead with our climb the next day. We started before daylight, and followed a well-worn path from our camp to the lower slope of the volcano and started upward. We passed the tree line at about 13,500 feet and snow line soon thereafter. At first, the climb was not too difficult because it was just a steep slope (ca 25 to 30°), but as we got higher all this changed, and the sky became deep purple rather than blue. I noted a small area of bare rock off to the right so I moved over to examine it. As I got closer I saw movement on the surface, so I decided to check that out. Surprisingly it turned out to be two lizards (Montane Graphic Lizard, *Sceloporus grammicus*) on an area of rock completely surrounded by snow and ice! The dark rock surface was warm, however, and it must have attracted enough insects to sustain these lizards. As it neared noon we decided to eat, and that was our undoing. Both my climb mates had brought along peanut butter and jelly sandwiches, while I had brought only sweetened fluids. We continued to climb for a short time after "lunch", but we were now so high that we could take only about ten steps before we had to stop and gasp for breath for several moments before we could take ten more steps! My climb mates then stopped. I don't know how high we were then, but would guess perhaps between 15 to 16 thousand feet (airliners, before pressurized cabins, typically went on oxygen at 10,000 feet). My colleagues had both become sick after eating lunch, and didn't want to continue. I wasn't sick, but I did not want to continue on alone, so we all turned around, sat down on our butts, and slid down to the snow line far below. I learned later that such fatty foods as peanut butter can't be easily digested at such elevations.

COMMENTARY
by WILLIAM RETZLAFF

I am extremely pleased to be able to pen some comments on Ralph Axtell's vignettes. My purpose is to provide the reader with the incentive to explore the history of SIUE throughout the chapters in this volume and those of the previous volume. I was extremely fortunate to be asked to join the faculty in the Department of Biological Sciences and the Environmental Sciences Program at SIUE in 1999. Saying "yes" was the smartest career decision I have ever made. I still remember being greeted by Ralph at my interview, and marveling at the fact that he had been an SIUE faculty member for 40+ years. I've learned a lot from Ralph and from some of the other faculty and authors in this volume. During my stay at SIUE, I had the wonderful experience of being the President of The Nature Preserve Foundation and looking after John and Kay Kendall's extraordinary jewel in Edwardsville, The Watershed Nature Center. I served on The Nature Preserve Foundation Board with Max Gricevich (one of the students that Ralph highlights in his vignette about early field trips). I've always felt that a person's experiences and those of his colleagues help define their role in life. Like you, after reading Ralph's vignettes, I wonder what would have happened if the shot had brought the helicopter down, or if the humble, tumultuous beginnings had lead to another name or a different institutional style. I'm glad it did not, as I love SIUE. I am passionate about its history and what the future holds. I was once asked about Ralph's contribution to the Department of Biological Sciences (while I was Department Chair) by a previous Dean. I replied "Ralph just published a book, had a lizard named after him, and was recognized for his lifetime achievements by the American Herpetological Society". Many of the other authors in this volume have had similar experiences and I know that I have learned from reading about them.

I too, like other SIUE faculty, have memories and experiences to relate, though telling most of them here would be beyond the scope of this volume; nevertheless, a few small recollections are relevant to this volume. Not too long ago, I was with my students at a professional meeting in Minneapolis, MN. During the late afternoon poster session I noticed a distinguished, older gentleman asking a lot of questions of my students about the work that the students had completed for their project. I stayed in the background (as a good mentor does initially), but soon realized that the questions from the gentleman were ones of familiarity. He finally revealed to the students that he had worked at SIUE during the early years. He commented on our new logo, the cougar head, on their poster and talked about SIU "at" Edwardsville fondly. My students were impressed, not only was this gentleman knowledgeable of their research work, he knew the place. I'm not sure of my memory, but this gentleman may have also been one of the early graduates at SIUE. During his senior year in high school his part-time job was to guard the student records in one of the old farmhouses (that Ralph mentions in his vignettes above) between the hours of 2:00 and 8:00 am. Incredible. This gentleman told us that he had gone on to receive a Ph.D. from the University of Iowa, worked there, and recently retired. He knew of the SIUE "helicopter incident" and the old horse track on campus and many of the other "stories" I had heard of SIUE's early beginnings. My students couldn't believe when he recounted the long walks to class from North University Drive and that parking was worse in the early 1960's (no parking lots) than it is today. During our protracted conversation, our new "friend" also asked me about some of the older faculty on campus and I was able to recount some of the tales I had heard which he verified. I hope that a copy of this volume makes it way to him so that he can read about some of the experiences and relive them with those that he knew.

I'm proud to say that I have known and worked with Ralph Axtell and many other students, staff, and faculty at SIUE. I'm also proud to say that I work at an institution that values the past and looks to the future. I state unequivocally that my impressions of SIUE match Ralph's. When I arrived 13 years ago, SIUE was an extraordinary place, built upon a past that arose from the dreams and effort of myriad local citizens, administrators, staff, students, and passionate faculty. I'm happy to say that SIUE is still an extraordinary place. The stories from the authors in this book and the previous volume only scratch the surface. Enjoy the following stories!

the JOURNEY

by WILLIAM GRIVNA

"NordEast" Minneapolis is a long way from China. Back in the 1940's and '50's there were no Chinese people there, and no "black people" either. NorthEast, or NordEast, as it was locally and affectionately called, was a small-town Polish/Russian/Scandinavian community within the larger, more urban city of Minneapolis, and just east of the Mississippi River. It was the kind of community in which you could listen to the baseball game from continuous porch radios just by walking down the street. It was also my hometown. Today, NordEast is a unique, semi-trendy arts and dining area recently written up in the NY Times. From NordEast Minneapolis to P.R.China, a long and rewarding journey into multi-culturalism and diversity. Much of the journey was enhanced or made possible by my nearly thirty year teaching career in the Department of Theater/Dance at SIUE.

In 1987, while directing a South African play for the St. Louis Black Repertory Company, I recruited my 19 year-old Asst. Stage Manager to become a student in the Theater/Dance Dept at SIUE. Several years later, when that same African-American female was a Junior level student in my Directing class, she publicly accused the literature content of my class (the omission of "famous" black theatre directors) as being racist. I was shocked. At that time there were relatively few highly influential, professional African-American theatre directors. Yet there were some. It simply had not occurred to me to include them amongst the major white directors historically. Her point was valid.

Thus began an even deeper awareness in me of "white privilege" and how consistent vigilance must be maintained to avoid even inadvertent racism. This personal journey eventually led me to an even larger multi-cultural perspective, both academically and artistically. All of my subsequent 25 years at SIUE had much to do with educating myself multi-culturally, and then sharing that knowledge and experiences with others—with students, other faculty, fellow artists, and with audiences. With the support of SIUE, I was able to obtain sabbaticals, developmental leaves, grants, and performance venues, in order to create new multi-cultural classes, explorations, productions, and projects.

Try tracking the causative events and random thoughts that lead to major life-changing experiences in your life. I've been studying and teaching T'ai Chi Ch'uan now for 35 years. I'm still a "beginner." T'ai Chi, like my Directing class' omission of black directors, was instrumental in leading my individual journey to greater awareness, interaction, and friendship with people of differing cultures. Rather than tracking the journey with a long list of strangely linked events, I'd simply like to share some personal anecdotes which may create a fuller and more engaging sense of both the insights and the delights of my journey.

"Wouldn't it be fun to live in, say, Paris for three months," a friend might ask. "Sure," you excitedly reply. "How about for six months?"

"Well, yes," you say, "that would be good too." "How about for a full year?" "Hmmm, I guess so, but that's really a long time," might be your more hesitant response. With that personal conversation in mind, what might it be like if you were to choose to give up your own country, and move to a new country forever? That's the question that all would-be immigrants must ask of themselves. It's not an easy question to answer. Leaving your family, friends, home, culture, and changing to a new language possibly for the rest of your life! The vast possibilities for home-sickness in ever-fluctuating manifestations are impossible to fully imagine.

During the course of an almost four-month long sabbatical in P.R. China, I experienced a bit of what that home-sickness might be like. First, I must say, that I hope that the playful, self-deprecating tales that follow do not paint me as a whining "ugly American," but rather serve as a reminder to all of us, that being alone in a different culture from one's own, can be alternately exciting and difficult, both pragmatically and emotionally.

I spent the majority of my time in China in Beijing and Shanghai at two of the most prestigious actor training programs in the country, the Traditional Theatre Institute in Beijing, and the Shanghai Theatre Academy. At the end of each research day, studying training/performance techniques and curriculum, my translators would go home to their families, and I would be alone to explore those remarkable cities. Speaking only a minimal number of Mandarin Chinese words and phrases, my alone-ness was amplified when my translators were gone. I would find myself going to more expensive western style hotels, with rooftop bars/restaurants, where international businessmen (who could speak English) would often materialize, also in search of post-work day camaraderie. That mutual drive seemed to be to find someone with whom to communicate all that we had experienced in, what was then, a quite different country, with its quite difficult language and culture. In 1990, China's massive movement toward an even greater "modernization" had not yet materialized. It was only one year after the "Tiananmen Square Turmoil."

One Sunday, after several months in China, I decided to forego my usual "on-the-go" Chinese breakfast foods, and treat myself to a western-style brunch buffet at a big international hotel. Ahhh, omelettes, eggs benedict, bacon, fresh squeezed orange juice, with chocolate sundaes for dessert! It was wonderful! (A far cry from bean-paste pastries, dumplings, and tea, though I actually enjoy Chinese food immensely.) Feeling happily sated, I decided to go to one of Beijing's very few public, direct-dial telephones, at that time, and call some friends in America, to hear familiar voices, and further celebrate the day.

It must be noted that without a direct-dial phone, and with a 12 hour time-zone difference, and having to go through a Chinese operator who often spoke "no English," and me with essentially "no Chinese," making phone calls to America was daunting, to say the least, and often seemed frustratingly impossible. But, with my smiling stomach, I ventured forth by crowded bus, far across the city, to the Beijing Fandian (hotel) to make my "salvational" call to English-speaking friends in the good ol' USA. I struck out! Three separate phone calls with "no answer" and only one answering machine. Alone! In China for several months now, and selfishly feeling "abandoned" by friends. But, AT&T to the rescue! Much like a subsequent TV commercial, I apparently moaned and groaned loud enough to catch the American operator's attention. This sweet young woman asked me, "Sir, what's wrong? Where are you?" I probably rambled a bit incoherently, but got out the basic facts. I had been in China for quite awhile, was lonely, and none of my friends in America that I had just called were at home. Then, this wonderful AT&T angel said, "Sir, I'll talk to you for a few minutes," and she did. We did. We talked in English. I have no recollection of what we said, but she made me smile, and get teary-eyed, all at the same time. It seemed profound! I probably asked her to marry me. After a few minutes she said that she had to go. I thanked her thoroughly, and left the hotel with a gladdened heart. I even drank a rarely found, at the time, can of actual Coke before leaving.

Speaking of food and beverage, another of my most vivid recollections had to do with cans of Campbell's soup. At some point, also in Beijing, probably in another hotel bar (easier to talk there than in a museum) I met a fellow from the American Embassy, who indicated that he was CIA, and who tipped me off to another restaurant/bar that all the Embassy employees frequented. Though the owners were Chinese, they apparently served "real hamburgers, with real mustard and ketchup." I met him there once, and the beer and burgers were good. The patrons were fun too. This same Embassy fellow also told me about a truly western-style Holiday Inn Hotel on the outskirts of Beijing, which had a 7-Eleven type of store in its basement. I should go there he said. On another Sunday afternoon, I did just that. It was a long trolley ride, almost to the airport. It was worth it! After wandering about the relative splendor of this Holiday Inn, compared to the many Soviet style block-like buildings of the time in China, I made my way downstairs to what became my "7-Eleven Wonderland." After three months of eating Chinese food, as good as it is, for every single meal (including breakfast), I suddenly saw shelf after shelf of familiar comfort food (which seemed at that moment like gustatory delights). Macaroni and cheese in a box, cans of tuna, and yes, can after can of Campbell's soup. Tears came to my eyes. I don't even eat Campbell's soup, but I bought some anyway. I can't even remember consuming them. Perhaps I just put them on a small shelf, and used them as an icon to dream of America, finally donating them to a friend/translator when I eventually left the country.

Speaking of leaving the country, I must tell you about one of my translators in Shanghai and how he helped me leave China on the first of my visits. His name was Zhang Yunian, and he was, at that time, the Asst. Dean of Performing Arts at The Shanghai Theatre Academy. He was also a professional actor, and looked and acted at least ten years younger than his thirty-six years. His was a deep, impassioned soul, but not without a great sense of fun. Be our discussions on art, philosophy, or politics (we had to be careful on that one), he and we laughed a lot! Even serious situations could bring

Zhang Yunian (friend and interpreter) and Bill Grivna (at SIUE about 1988).
PHOTOGRAPHER UNKNOWN.

out Yunian's teasing playfulness. On that first visit, my work was completed a few weeks early, and I wanted to change my plane ticket for an earlier departure. (Besides, it would not be politically wise to be wandering about China, one year after the "Tiananmen Square Turmoil" without an official organizational sponsor.) So, my trusty translator and friend, Yunian, sought to help me arrange a change in plane reservations. All the local travel agents we tried were somehow unable to help, other than for a seemingly exorbitant increase in fare. Yunian would have none of that. We kept trying. Finally, after a repeat visit to the same agent, the man (somewhat mysteriously) implied that "if" I did go early to the airport the next day, and asked for such and such flight, I would perhaps get on with stand-by. That seemed "iffy." What to do? Yunian felt that it was worth a try.

By the time we finally got back to my room at the Theatre Academy, it was already evening, and I would still have to pack. The room had two twin beds, and while I wrestled frantically with slamming clothes, notebooks, gifts, toothpaste, etc., into several bags on one bed, Yunian decided to lighten the situation by singing traditional Chinese folk-songs and Chinese opera at the top of his lungs, while flinging himself up and down on the opposite bed, and laughing heartily throughout. He was great. Somehow my nerves were calmed and I finished my packing. We agreed to meet early the next morning, and he would see me off in a cab, giving instructions to the driver for the airport. Suffice it to say, I managed to get some nervous sleep, say farewell to my friend Yunian in the morning (perhaps never to see him again), get to the airport on time, and successfully catch the plane.

Time lapse. Three years later, after a second trip to China in 1991, and much correspondence and many plans, a number of which did not come to fruition, I had managed to "sponsor" Zhang Yunian to come to America to teach Acting at SIUE, while pursuing a Master's degree in Mass Communications. Side note. On my leave-taking from that second visit to China, I had again stayed briefly at the Shanghai Theatre Academy. On my departure night, again a slightly hurried one, I gave Yunian about $60.00 in American money to pay for my room. Flash forward to May 19, 1993. I drive to the St. Louis airport to pick up Yunian. His wife and 7-year-old daughter are not able to follow him for another six months. The first thing Yunian did, after we exchanged a big hug, was hand me ten Chinese Yuan, the equivalent of the two American dollars he had received in change for paying my room rent in Shanghai two years previously!

Another time lapse. Yunian's personal journey has led him from interning at WSIE, our campus radio station, to The Voice of America radio in Washington D.C, to Chinese Language teaching, to a Master's degree in Special Ed, which he now teaches in Fairfax VA. He is currently training to be an Assistant Principal. It was a proud moment for both of us, when he achieved his American Citizenship. It was an even prouder moment for me, several years later, when he called to ask for my approval to name his new American born son after me.

Culture switch. My personal experience in China, with Asian Theatre, culture, and relationships, all during situations in which I was clearly "the other," increased my appreciation of the difficulties of being "the other" by anyone else, in any new cultural setting. During the 1980's and '90's, the African-American presence on our SIUE campus seemed to grow increasingly larger. In the earlier stages of this development, our Black students, in my view, did not yet have much of a "voice," especially in the Department of Theater/Dance. In 1996, the Office for Cultural and Social Diversity was created, and much great work was done by Assistant Provost Rudy Wilson and his office. New opportunities were created. New connections were made. There was an increase in the number of African-American, as well as some African, faculty members. Organizations developed. Voices were heard. An institutional commitment was made to create funding for the recruitment and hiring of minority faculty. We had been understaffed in the Performance Area of the Theater/Dance department for many years. My frequent complaints about this situation fell, by chance, on the ears of SIUE Associate Provost David Sill, a former Chair of our Department. David suggested that we try to find a half-time African-American teacher/actor to teach several introductory performance courses. He would help to find the funding for the position. He did. We did. First, we hired one of our former theater students, Robert Mitchell, who was by then an established professional actor in St. Louis. Later, we hired Lisa Colbert, also a professional actor, who, within a few brief years, became a wonderful and beloved full-time teacher, and with whom I co-created the "Multi-Cultural Theater in America" class. Lisa also created the popular, and annual, "Black Theater Workshop". Then tragedy struck. Lisa had a sudden and untimely death from a seemingly dormant illness. After recovering from our great loss, we were finally able to hire our current full-time Asst. Professor in that same position, Ms. Kathryn Bentley, who has since been with our department for five full and highly productive years.

Now, here's the great "magic, full-circle," to the beginnings of my multi-cultural journey via SIUE. Prof. Bentley is one and the same person who was the young African-American student, mentioned at the beginning of this chapter, whom I recruited to SIUE and who challenged my Directing course as being "racist." "Full circle number two" is the fact that in 1989 I wrote a letter of recommendation for Kathryn Bentley for the SIUE Martin Luther King Jr. Student of the Year Award. She won! It gets better. In 2009, I wrote another letter of recommendation for Kathryn Bentley, this time for the Martin Luther King Jr. Humanitarian Award for Faculty. She won again! I could not be more proud of Prof. Bentley, both for her individual accomplishments, and for all that she represents, which is the enormous growth

Bill Grivna and Prof. Kathryn Bentley.
PHOTOGRAPH BY HERBERT BENTLEY.

of SIUE as an institution that is fully committed to a Multi-cultural and International world-view. It's been a wonderful, growth-producing journey for me as well. And I'm happy to say that even "NordEast" Minneapolis has a significant multi-cultural and international community now.

One final tale...something worth remembering. Soon after his arrival at SIUE, Zhang Yunian was taking a course in which, ironically as it turns out, a seemingly simple multi-cultural assignment was given by the Instructor. Rent a certain Bruce Lee video, and write a brief paper noting cultural differences. Simple enough. But, here's a few, unfortunately over-looked, culturally "biased" factors:

1) Yunian lived in student housing at Tower Lake. He had no transportation to Edwardsville to find a video store.
2) He had no idea where any video stores were, or what times they were open.
3) A video rental then was $2.00. In China, two American dollars equaled ten Chinese dollars (yuan), a fair amount of money to someone who as a graduate teaching assistant was only making $ 360 per month.
4) Renting a video required an ID.

Well, our intrepid, resourceful and dauntless "warrior," Yunian, was determined to fulfill the task. On a Saturday morning, early, he borrowed a bicycle. He somehow figured out a pedal-path to downtown Edwardsville. He arrived about 8:30 a.m., when many stores are open in China. Video stores in Edwardsville were not. He waited. It didn't open. By asking a passer-by, he discovered that there was another video store "at the other end" of Hwy 159. He had no idea how far that was from downtown, but he was pointed in the right direction, and he took off. It was summer time. It was already hot. He was sweating hard, but he got there. It was about 9:30 a.m. now. The sign said that the store would open at 10 a.m. He waited. It got hotter. Finally, the store opened. He went inside, searched the titles (in his non-native English) and eventually found the required Bruce Lee video. He went to the checkout counter with his two dollars in hand and the video…feeling like a success. "Let's see your ID," said the clerk. "ID? What ID?" His only legal ID at this early point in his arrival was his passport, and it was all the way back at Tower Lake. "Your Driver's License?" suggested the clerk helpfully. "Sorry," he didn't have one. "I'm sorry," said the clerk, "I can't let you rent the video without an ID."

Nearly defeated, Yunian had one final "desperate" hope. Maybe if he contacted the instructor, something could be done. I don't remember how he got the phone number, was he carrying the syllabus with him, so as not to make a mistake in the name of the required video? The clerk let him use the store phone. The instructor's wife answered the phone. The instructor was not at home. Yunian's "tale of woe" came tumbling out. The wife, another "angel," volunteered to drive to the store and rent the video for him. She did. Yunian wrote a good paper. I expect that even with his wife's recounting of the event, the instructor never fully comprehended all the cultural difficulties he had created with his "simple" multi-cultural assignment. Ahhh, yes, vigilance…

Cast of SIUE Multi-cultural production of *Rowing to America*.
PHOTOGRAPH BY C. OTIS SWEEZY.

The Simultaneous Pursuit of Passions and Paychecks— It Can Be Done!

by SHEILA VOSS

Say what you will about the sketchy employment fates of liberal arts undergrads. From the moment I got that diploma, I have been gainfully employed, despite the doubts of my peers who assuredly took the accountant-law school-MBA route. And for the record, only a handful of those first paychecks required me to balance a serving tray.

Before seeking out SIUE, I had put my English/Communications degree from Pennsylvania State University to work in a rather meandering way. From spending a summer in the belly of the Library of Congress doing research on women's reproductive rights to fact-checking aviation articles for McGraw-Hill to writing ads for an ambulance manufacturer, those first few gigs out of the gate paid the rent but didn't quite fulfill. Something was amiss—a something-bigger, more-than-a-paycheck reason worth my time.

So while still in my mid-twenties, I set my sights on something *genuinely* bigger—killer whales. Determined to merge my childhood-driven passion for wildlife with my professional pursuits, I took a lesser-paying post as a science writer for SeaWorld Orlando's Education Department and simultaneously enrolled at the University of Central Florida to pursue a Master's degree in science education. Little did I know at the time that my lifelong vocation—**inspiring as many people as possible to celebrate, connect with, and conserve the natural world**—had officially begun.

During the day, I wrote marine ecology curricula, gave behind-the-scenes tours of our sea turtle rescue area, and worked with teachers, students and scientists. At night, I dove into courses on learning theory, educational technology, and evolutionary biology. On weekends, I got SCUBA-certified and volunteered at a local raptor rehabilitation facility, perfecting my technique of swiftly killing mice for hungry hawks. While fairly broke, I felt invigorated and constantly curious. I was doing stuff I cared about…and I got good at it.

Soon, SeaWorld invited me to serve its St. Louis-based parent company Busch Entertainment Corporation, a move that put my near-finished M.A. degree on indefinite hold. Upon moving to St. Louis to handle environmental communications and education programs for six zoological parks across the country, I felt overwhelmed and out of my league. As I dug deep into my work, however, that changed. I was constantly on the road, helping develop entirely new animal exhibits, forging national conservation partnerships, launching public awareness campaigns, and even winning an Emmy for a children's television production about rescuing penguins from a South Africa oil spill. I was having fun and, once again, getting good at my craft.

But after a few short years in my new post, I experienced that same gut-check twinge I felt back in my copywriting days—something was amiss. This time, however, it wasn't lack of purpose or passion. It was lack of details. As I harvested tidbits of content from the world of science for my projects and productions, whether the focus was marine ecology, ocean conservation, or threats to endangered species, I found myself wanting to dive deeper. I wanted to understand the complex, sometimes-arcane science behind the stories, and ultimately share that science in relevant, compelling ways with an audience of millions. The world and every organism in it, I was convinced, would be far better off if more humans truly knew how the natural world worked. While still keeping my day job, I decided soon after to go back to school.

By this point, I was less interested in neatly wrapping up my science education degree and more interested in science itself. Moreover, I was intrigued with the interplay between science and real-world social, political and economic decisions. While researching my options, I looked into programs at other institutions of higher learning across the greater St. Louis region, but it was SIUE's Environmental Sciences M.S. program—with its appealing mix of natural sciences and social sciences—that got my attention.

Able to salvage a few UCF transfer credits, I honed in on the program's Public Administration and Policy tract, diving into courses like advanced environmental sciences, applied ecology, conservation biology, statistics, communicating research, environmental policy, and environmental law. Because I worked full-time, my SIUE experience consisted of evening and weekend classes over a few years. While not the same dynamic as a relatively carefree undergraduate studying, living and playing on campus, my time there had plenty of collegial moments. From convening our group project team in the campus coffee spot for a semester's worth of Saturdays to critiquing the newest reading assignments in downtown's Stagger Inn, I always felt like I was amid fellow knowledge-seekers who were there to learn.

Like many who go back to school while working full time, my stake in the program was significant. My SIUE nights and weekends became a much-needed outlet for critical thinking, informed debate, and knowledge-building. Some of my work-life challenges cathartically found their way into a few essays and other work assignments—only occasionally raising the eyebrows of a professor or two. Negotiating

Sheila often sneaks science words and concepts into everyday outdoor play, whether that's climbing a deciduous tree, discovering a chrysalis, eye-spying for predators and prey, or digging for decomposers.

PHOTOGRAPH BY KATE VOSS.

my corporate life during the day and plugging away at coursework at night, I became increasingly fascinated and frustrated with the raging knowledge gap between natural science experts and decision-makers in the public, private and business sectors. I recall struggling with the reality that so many financial decisions are made without fully accounting for impacts to water, air, soil, plants and animals. Regardless of the course, this theme found its way into more and more of my essays, some more caustic than others. My professors began to notice the trend, and soon were shepherding me toward what would be two intense years of inquiry, interviews, struggles and success.

With the support of my SIUE professors and Anheuser-Busch colleagues, I focused my masters' thesis on the relationship between corporate environmental and financial performance. While successful companies have always conducted long-term financial planning, they traditionally have not fully accounted for environmental impacts and opportunities. Short-term returns on investment and quick paybacks are preferred, often leading to future unaccounted-for costs down the road. As I began my research, from investigating energy policies to documenting environmental accounting trends to attempting to understand the science of energy production, I found myself being pulled in many tangential directions. With the guidance of my trusted SIUE advisor Dr. Jacky So, I began to focus further.

Blending the fields of public policy, technology and corporate finance, my study eventually zeroed in on a potential energy investment—cogeneration—at one of Busch Entertainment's California-based facilities. Specifically, it analyzed two different investment options (cogenerated power/25% grid reliance or purchased power/100% grid reliance), then applied two different methodologies—traditional investment analysis and something called "Total Cost Assessment," or TCA. TCA accounted for significantly more variables, including natural resource availability, state and federal legislative actions, technology advances, social considerations, conservation concerns, consumer preferences, and more. The findings: While both TCA and standard financial analysis favored investing in cogeneration over a 15-year investment horizon, TCA resulted in a greater "total cost" profile variance between the two options, further favoring the cogeneration investment versus total grid reliance. Translation: When "externalities" like natural resources are factored into long-term investment decisions, the more resource-efficient scenario will not only protect resources, but also cost less.

Looking back, what sticks with me most about my thesis investigation is that I wasn't an energy expert. I wasn't an accountant. I wasn't an engineer. I wasn't a public policy expert. But yet, I had to pull on all those areas of expertise to get clarity and a comprehensive understanding of what was at stake. Think of how we work today. Think of all the decisions made—big and small—that don't fully account for impacts to the environment upon which we all rely. What if more people in all professions—accountant, engineer, doctor, CEO, journalist, artist, parent, teacher, lawyer, construction worker, video game maker, waitress and Wall Street trader—had a solid, science-based understanding of how the natural world works and of our total reliance on it for our very survival. Now imagine if that understanding and appreciation was the basic starting-point for all their decisions. For both scientists and non-scientists to more fully know the wonders of science, the limits of science, the dangers of ignoring or misapplying it, and why it's done in the first place could be transformative on so many levels.

In late 2009, after 15 fantastic, hard and adventurous years, I left Busch Entertainment to join Missouri Botanical Garden as its Vice President of Education. Here, I get to continue doing what I was doing for the zoo and aquarium world, but for one of the world's most renowned botanical gardens. In addition to the main Garden near downtown St. Louis, I now work with and for Shaw Nature Reserve (Gray Summit, MO), the Sophia M. Sachs Butterfly House (Chesterfield, MO), Litzsinger Road Ecology Center (Ladue, MO) and the impressive MBG network of global science and conservation projects active in more than 30 countries. I've joined a stellar staff committed to engaging a diversity of visitors, increasing knowledge, broadening perspectives, sparking curiosity, and fostering a lifelong love and stewardship of the natural world. Admittedly, engaging the visiting public about furry creatures is far easier. But the dramatic, shocking, humbling and wondrous world of plants holds a treasure trove of Emmy-worthy stories just waiting to be told.

While my work palette has changed a bit, I'm still pouring my energies into activities worth something to me—inspiring visitors of all ages, backgrounds and abilities to explore their world, understand how it works, appreciate its wonders, and act in ways that protect it for generations to come. In this role, I've enjoyed reconnecting with SIUE on a whole new level—as partner institutions aiming to strengthen our shared St. Louis community while also setting our sights on worthy, global goals. I'm once again having fun...and hopefully will get better as I go.

The Gardens at SIUE are among the favorite destinations of Sheila and her family, including daughter Kate and son Will.

PHOTOGRAPH BY STEVEN VOSS.

As for SIUE's role in all of this, I will forever be grateful. My SIUE graduate experience was truly life-altering. For one, the natural beauty of the campus and the small, classic town of Edwardsville was hard to resist. Now calling Edwardsville home since 2002, my little family and I frequent *The Gardens at SIUE* and the SIUE campus as if they were extensions of our own backyard. We bike its trails, enjoy Dunham Hall's Children's Theatre, sip Pike Place brew at its Student Center Starbucks, and take in a Cougar basketball game now and then.

Thank you SIUE, for your pivotal role in one of my life's gut-check moments: for broadening my perspective, for strengthening my knowledge, and for being among the greatest backyards ever. The generations of learners you've shepherded, and those to come, better the world we all share.

For Further Reading

Bell, P. and B. Lewenstein, A.W. Shouse, M.A. Feder, eds. 2009. *Learning Science in Informal Environments. People, Places, and Pursuits.* Washington, D.C.: The National Academies Press.

Borchelt, R. and K. Hudson. 2008. "Engaging the Scientific Community with the Public," *Science Progress.*

Falk, J. and Dierking, L. 2010. The 95 percent solution: School is not where Americans learn most of their science. *American Scientist 98* (6).

McCallie, E., Bell, L., Lohwater, T., Falk, J.H., Lehr, J.L., Lewenstein, B.V., Needham, C., and Wiehe, B. 2009. "Many Experts, Many Audiences: Public Engagement with Science and Informal Science Education"—A CAISE Inquiry Group Report. Center for Advancement of Informal Science Education.

Meinwald, J. and J.G. Hildebrand, eds. 2010. *Science and the Educated American: A Core Component of Liberal Education.* Cambridge, MA: American Academy of Arts & Sciences.

Tellus Institute. 1992. *Total Cost Assessment: Accelerating Industrial Pollution Prevention Through Innovative Project Financial Analysis.* Washington, D.C.: US Environmental Protection Agency.

Todd, R. 1994. *Zero Loss Environmental Accounting Systems.* Pp 191-200 in The Greening of Industrial Ecosystems, B.R. Allenby and D.J. Richards, eds. National Academy of Engineering. Washington D.C.: The National Academies Press.

Reflections

by JACK G. SHAHEEN

When you part from a friend, you grieve not; For that which you love most in him may be clearer in his absence, as the mountain to the climber is clearer from the plain. —KAHLIL GIBRAN

Beginnings

A thin sheet of ice covered the winding pavement alongside our home on Creasy Springs Road in Columbia, Missouri. It was mid-February 1969. This cold, bleak, wet morning was to become the most important day of my academic future. I jump-started the day at around 4 am. Why this early? I had to prepare for my first formal teaching interview, at Southern Illinois University Edwardsville (SIUE).

As a PhD candidate at the University of Missouri, I eagerly anticipated flying into St. Louis and visiting the SIUE campus. After gulping two cups of black coffee and eating some stale oat bran cereal, I put on my finest suit and tie, grabbed my overcoat, kissed my wife

Bernice goodbye, and rushed out the door of our modest rental home. A freezing rain storm was in full force so I drove ever so carefully to our postage-size airport. Not surprisingly, on arrival I was told my flight to Lambert Field was canceled. Not to fret, announced the airline agent; a retired school bus was en route to deliver us to Lambert. Because the roads were treacherous, most airline passengers opted to return to their homes. Not me. I, along with four other fool-hardy souls, leaped onto the creaky bus. I decided to brave the icy I 70 highway for one reason—I did not want to miss meeting and being interviewed by my host, Professor John Rider, Chairman of the Mass Communications Department. Though I had received several offers to teach at universities from California to Missouri, SIUE ranked at the very top of my list. I was excited.

Unbeknownst to Prof. Rider, in early January I had donned my black fedora and went undercover. Pretending to be a prospective student, I drove from Columbia to SIUE to check out the campus, asking selected students and faculty members whether SIUE was a good place to be. The vote was practically unanimous. The major complaints: No gymnasium—in order to jog two miles we had to circle a hastily erected, leaky and inflatable bubble gym, over and over again. Plus, there were no swimming pools. So, we were obliged to glub-glub in the polluted waters of Tower Lake. There was lack of housing, only one major grocery store, and some grouchy local residents who complained about "those university people taking over the town." Yet, for many reasons SIUE was where I belonged.

But could I arrive safely for my interview with Prof. Rider? En route, there were dozens of accidents complete with police and ambulance sirens; numerous cars and trucks were abandoned in roadside ditches along interstate 70. Eventually, our putt-putt school bus pulled up at the St. Louis airport, four hours past my scheduled flight arrival time. As the bus sputtered to a halt, there was Rider, curbside at the airport, waiting to greet me. "Welcome Jack," he smiled; "so glad you made it." From that moment on, I was hooked.

John Rider was ahead of his time. He helped shape the future of media education by establishing a Mass Communications Department, not a Journalism School or a Radio-TV-Film unit. In the 1960s, students attending universities with Journalism schools were limited to taking courses in print journalism. If they wanted to study Radio, Television or Film, they were obliged to go to another Department, and vice-versa. And many of those departments were at odds with each other, making it difficult for students to study both Print and Broadcast Journalism. On several occasions, Rider's innovative, liberal thinking was contested, both on and off campus, especially by traditional schools of Journalism, such as the University of Missouri.

Our students were free to take as many or as few print and/or electronic media courses they wanted to, all in the same department. Upon graduation, they received degrees in Mass Communications. In addition to their course work, they took advantage of numerous hands-on opportunities. They could work as reporters, photographers and editors with the campus newspaper, the *Alestle*. They could

Jack Shaheen with students outside the Fine Arts Building.
PHOTOGRAPH COURTESY OF PHOTOGRAPHIC SERVICES COLLECTION, UNIVERSITY ARCHIVES, LOVEJOY LIBRARY.

also work at and help program WSIE-FM, our on-campus National Public Radio (NPR) affiliate. Finally, students could develop television skills with our state-of-the-art TV facility, a facility which housed equipment as up-to date as most St. Louis TV stations. SIUE was the place to be, not only because of its new facilities and its practical approach to media education—it was the place to be because of John Rider's warmth and leadership.

Rider always encouraged his colleagues to excel. He gave me the freedom to conduct research and to teach effectively. As a fresh PhD graduate, I was not yet aware of my teaching strengths and weaknesses. This is why I rejected offers from more-established universities; they wanted me to teach the same courses, year in, year out. Rider, however, gave me the opportunity to grow. I taught several different courses, from "Introduction to Mass Communications" to "Criticism in the Public Arts," until I eventually discovered those classes where I excelled. I then went on to guide my students to absorb knowledge from texts related to broadcasting research, history and ethics.

Then there was our dynamic leader, President John Rendleman; the only university president to greet and interview me. Indeed, he interviewed all the candidates. His solid, enduring commitment to SIUE was contagious. Rendleman treated students, staff and faculty as individuals, not as numbers. His office door was always open, no appointments necessary. If an SIUE "family" member had been wrongly slighted, he would be there to help her/him.

One memorable example: My dear friends, Professor Kamil Winter, and his wife Doralice, had recently escaped communist Russia's occupation of what was then Czechoslovakia. Yet, for months they had serious difficulties with a Chicago immigration officer, in spite of the fact that both had served alongside allied forces during World War II, and both had vigorously spoken out against the Russian occupation. Though they made several trips to Chicago to plead their case, the officer persisted. Believing the Winters to be evil communists, she was about to ship them back. When Kamil confided in me about his dilemma, I promptly called Rendleman at his home. He was immersed in watching a Monday Night football game, so he wasn't particularly pleased to be dragged away from the TV set to speak with a faculty member about a university problem. But he did.

The following morning, he summoned Kamil Winter to his office. Here, one of Rendleman's legal associates ushered Kamil into an adjacent room. He gathered the facts about the immigration situation, and then made several phone calls. Within a few days the Winter case was successfully resolved. Several years later, my wife Bernice and I proudly witnessed a beautiful ceremony at the Belleville courthouse declaring Kamil and Doralice citizens of the United States, thanks to John Rendleman.

Colleagues

This Arab proverb applies to my fellow teachers, "One hand alone cannot clap." During my tenure at the university, several faculty members reached out to support my research on the Arab stereotype as well as help shape my life—Kamil Winter, for one. Saturdays I would meet him downtown Edwardsville for coffee and conversation at "the" restaurant noted for its piping hot java and yummy pies—Jesse's Café. Each morning he gave me invaluable research advice, and then we went on to solve the world's problems. Winter's teaching skills extended beyond the classroom; he educated a secret admirer on international politics; a local resident. A few years after Jesse's Café closed its doors, I was introduced to this lady. She confessed that every Saturday she would seek us out by going to Jesse's and sitting in the booth next to ours. Here, she would listen attentively to that "brilliant man from Europe." She said that she was upset when Jesse's closed its doors; she did not know where we'd gone. "We moved to Jack-in-the-Box, where coffee was free for seniors," I said. "No wonder I couldn't find you," she puffed, "no one drinks that coffee."

Our university's cafeteria, however, perked some hearty java; a single cup kept one awake throughout the day, and at night, too. It was here that I befriended another mentor, English Professor Robert Duncan. At 7:30 am sharp, we opened the cafeteria; we were the first in line. I brought my own ceramic cup with me, and heated it with boiling hot water. We also consumed some freshly baked chocolate-nut covered donuts—the tastiest donuts ever. Occasionally, I'd treat the family, bringing a dozen or so to our home. One morning the cashier decided to charge me extra because my cup was "so big." Bob rescued me, explaining that I saved the university money by not using one of their styrofoam cups. Like me, Duncan was a Steelers-Pirate fan. He, too, was born in a steel town, McKeesport, Pa., just a few miles from my home in Clairton. In his youth, Bob excelled in journalism, working as a reporter for the McKeesport Daily News. During our morning coffee-donut sessions he would help improve my writing skills. Bob would take several new, sharp pencils with erasers, and would work tirelessly with me on my academic essays, my opinion editorials and my weekly TV column for the East St. Louis Journal. Thanks to Bob's patience, constructive guidance, and friendship, editors of journals, and newspapers such as the *St. Louis Post-Dispatch* and the *Washington Post*, welcomed my writings.

Due in part to the now defunct Faculty Club, I was able to forge lasting friendships with many other faculty members, notably Chemistry's Michael Matta, Journalism's William Ward, Speech's Robert Hawkins, Music's Leonard Van Camp, Art's David Huntley, and Political Science's Richard Millett. The Club's beautiful hilltop location along with its informal, intimate atmosphere helped create a spirit of innovation and commitment to the university. Throughout the 1970s and early 80's, we would gather at the Club to share dreams and chuckles while Susie, the ever-so-friendly chef, grilled the best hamburgers in town. Susie was also a dear friend; she helped me with my first major on-campus interdisciplinary project—a Nuclear War Films series. When I told her that I was in search of a quiet place to work on this series she offered me an upstairs room at the Club, complete with an unlimited supply of smiles and hot java. Eventually, we screened and discussed six nuclear films in the Fine Arts building.

The nuclear series featured speakers from different departments: Physics, Chemistry and Sociology. Their edited comments were published in the campus newspaper. Later, in the Fall of 1978, thanks to the encouragement of Bob Duncan and William Tudor, the SIU Press published my first book, Nuclear War Films, which was based on the on-campus series. It was the first ever book-length critical examination of Hollywood's nuclear genre; both faculty and students contributed essays. Programmers at the St. Louis Art Museum were enthusiastic; in October I agreed to host and discuss at the museum a total of 16 movies, full-length features, as well as documentaries and educational short films.

Like myself, my faculty friends viewed the future with optimism, in spite of some damaging, local prejudices. For example, when Education Chairman Deane Wiley found out that a nearby school district would not accept SIUE's African-American student teachers, Wiley quickly responded by uttering a few non-printable phrases. Then, he told the district they would never have any student teachers from SIUE until they changed their policy. Wiley was an outstanding leader, and a champion of civil rights.

William Ward, whose student Bill Plaschke went on to become an outstanding sports columnist for the Los Angeles Times, boasted, "Our students will be as good if not better than those attending the University of Missouri's journalism school." And they were. We developed an innovative mass communications internship program that was both meaningful and challenging. For our students, the internship program was an inspirational initiation to understanding what it was going to take to become a professional. Our media internships enabled many SIUE graduates to be with nearly every radio/TV station, and newspaper in the area. Our students inundated the St. Louis area with their various skills. One example: John Lena, a student in my TV writing class interned at Communico, a St. Louis Motion Picture company. Afterwards, Lena went on to complete his screenplay, "Daffodils," about the impact of noise pollution. Communico's President, Bob Senseman, was so impressed with Lena's work that

Tommy Smothers in Jack's morning class.
PHOTOGRAPH COURTESY OF PHOTOGRAPHIC SERVICES COLLECTION, UNIVERSITY ARCHIVES, LOVEJOY LIBRARY.

Communico purchased the rights and subsequently produced and released Lena's "Daffodils." One of my SIUE scrapbooks contains a photograph of a happy Lena receiving his check from Senseman; Rider and yours truly are in the background. Another student in my writing class, "Paul," wrote a compelling teleplay based on an existing TV series, Jack Lord's "Hawaii Five'O." Earlier that year, I had met and befriended Five'O's producer, Leonard Freeman. Refreshingly, Freeman welcomed receiving and considering our students' teleplays for possible production, so I sent him Paul's. Though Paul's script never made it to the airwaves, Freeman took time to personally write back, advising Paul how best to improve his writing skills.

Many of our students hailed from Madison County and other nearby areas. But, thanks to John Rider's connections with the Lutheran Hour's world-wide radio network, we attracted international students. Graduate students from Nigeria, India, Lebanon,

South Africa, Jordan, Ethopia and other nations, received their degrees from SIUE. The department's reputation attracted noted guest speakers who willingly came to the campus and shared thoughts—usually for travel expenses only, plus a very modest fee. Marshall Flaum, the executive producer and director of the compelling "Undersea World of Jacques Cousteau" documentary series, spoke to several classes, delivered a commencement address, received an honorary degree, and donated to the university a dozen-plus of his telling documentaries. We also hosted actor Tommy Smothers, Sir Howard Stringer, the former executive producer of CBS Reports' documentary unit, now Executive Chairman and CEO of Sony Corporation of America, and we welcomed the warm-hearted, brilliant animator Chuck "Roadrunner" Jones.

The Jones visit was a near-miss tragedy. Jones arrived early evening April 24, 1973, the day his animated special, "The Cricket in Times Square," debuted. We planned on dinner at our home, and then watch the special, together. But Jones first wanted to check into his room at the local Holiday Inn. To ensure his room was in order I escorted him to the door. But as soon as we opened the door we were held at gunpoint. A well-dressed individual calling himself, "The Candy Man," was inside Jones' room; he refused to drop his weapon, insisting we were thugs out to get him. I insisted we were not, that we were experiencing a "failure to communicate," and said the front desk made a serious error by double-booking the room. Still waving the pistol at us, he called and checked my story with the not-so-alert desk clerk. She put him on hold, and ever so slowly she reluctantly admitted she double-booked the room, that Mr. Jones was, indeed, the famous animator from Hollywood. Satisfied, Mr. "Candy" lowered his weapon and told us to "Get the hell out." We rushed to the front desk, grabbed the key for the proper room and went directly to Jones' room. I sat on the bed, next to Jones, for ten-plus minutes, until he stopped shaking.

Our students also benefited from local guest speakers. They provided additional insights into our profession; it was a called a

Prof Riley Maynard with NBC-TV Edwin Newman and Jack Shaheen.
PHOTOGRAPH COURTESY OF PHOTOGRAPHIC SERVICES COLLECTION, UNIVERSITY ARCHIVES, LOVEJOY LIBRARY.

profession back then, not a business. We hosted journalists like Dick Richmond from the St. Louis Post-Dispatch, General Managers of TV stations such as KMOV-TV's Allen Cohen, and on-air personalities like anchor Betsey Bruce and KMOX Radio's beloved news and sports professionals, Bob Hardy and Bob Costas. Hardy's daughter, Sandy, was one of my brightest students; and Costas went on to become an outstanding sports analyst/anchor for NBC-TV.

When I think back on my years at SIUE, I humbly acknowledge the assistance of my university colleagues. Their helping hands enabled me to write several books, to become a Fulbright scholar, a CBS news consultant on Middle East Affairs, and to specialize in contesting damaging stereotypes of racial and ethnic groups, notably Arabs. I also fondly recall, my wonderful students, of which many I am proud to call friends, today. To name a few: Peter Maer; Peter has a passion for fairness and accuracy in the newsroom; he is the CBS News White House Correspondent. Then there's the dynamic Six

Flags over Mid-America duo, Robert Kochan and Michael Paladin. For more than a decade, they ran this amusement park; they graciously took care of this writer and his family. Kochan's rise to the top wasn't easy. Before he became President of the noted St. Louis Marketing Firm, Kochan and Company, he worked at the park as a part-time street magician. To his credit, he never confessed how he did those magic tricks. And, there's the committed supporter of the university's Mass Communications Department, John Klobnak. Each and every year, Klobnak, Chairman and CEO of Laser Vision, now Chairman of Confluence Acquisition Partners, Inc, awards five scholarships to outstanding communications students.

My students and colleagues at SIUE impacted my life. Fond memories of many townspeople also endure; There's the town's fixture: Friendly, honest Jack Minner, whose mechanical expertise still shines. Sadly, some residents are no longer with us. People like Rusty's owner/chef, Louis Badalamenti; his gourmet skills and welcoming smiles ignited hearts. There is the Bank of Edwardsville's John Hunter; who managed all our accounts, gratis, during the two years I taught abroad as a Fulbright scholar. And, I will always remember the unspoken generosity of barber Tom Eaker, who silently helped families who were unable to pay for their children's hair cuts.

The camaraderie of my many Edwardsville friends, university colleagues and students continues to bring much joy, inspiration and faith into my life. I raise my hot cup of coffee to them. Bless them all!

Jack Shaheen
PHOTOGRAPH BY JOHN BRACKETT.

Ruth Slenczynska, THE PIANIST Who Took Her Future in Her Hands

Interview by
ALDEMARO ROMERO

Ruth Slenczynska is an American pianist who some consider the first real child prodigy since Mozart. Born in Sacramento, California in 1925, her father imposed a severe and abusive discipline on her since she was three years old. At the age of six she had her debut in Berlin and by the age of 7 she was performing at the Salle Pleyel in France with a full orchestra—the Paris Philharmonic. When she was 15, she stopped performing in public, and it was not until 1951 that she resumed a concert career and established herself as a pianist of flawless technique and incredible musical sensitivity. In 1964, she accepted a full-time position at Southern Illinois University Edwardsville (SIUE) as Artist-in-Residence, a title she retained until 1987. Ms. Slenczynska married Dr. James Kerr, a professor of Political Science at SIUE, in 1967. She published a book of memoirs entitled, *Forbidden Childhood*, which deals with life as a child prodigy, and a book on piano technique entitled, *Music at Your Fingertips: Aspects of Pianoforte Technique*.

Ruth Slenczynska at age four.
PHOTOGRAPH BY KATHLEEN DOUGAN.

AR: Your father was a strict disciplinarian who abused you both verbally and physically while financially exploiting your musical talent. When one looks at your story as you told it in *Forbidden Childhood*, one thinks of those parents that insist in pressuring their kids into following career paths, whether in music, sports, or whatever, with little regard to their personal well being. Do you have any words of advice to those parents?

> RS: Yes, I would recommend that those parents look far into the future, as far as they possibly can, and decide what might be appealing and useful to the world that their children could do because only in that way can they hope for their children to succeed. I came from parents who believed that their children have to follow in what the parents did. Consequently, my father thought because he was a musician, I had to be a musician, and thought only in terms of the way he was taught, that's the way I should be

Ruth Slenczynska publicity photo ca. 1955.
PHOTOGRAPH COURTESY OF PHOTOGRAPHIC SERVICES COLLECTION, UNIVERSITY ARCHIVES, LOVEJOY LIBRARY.

taught and I don't think that that is the way to go. I think that parents must look ahead, as far into the future as possible and try to direct their children to have dreams toward that future.

AR: If one of the people reading this right now is one of those kids being pressured by their parents to follow a particular career path, what would you say to him or her?

RS: Well, I would tell them that they should listen to their parents but that they should not upset their own dreams; that their own dreams are something that have great value and that could lead them further than possibly their parents could even expect from them. I believe that every individual is entitled to dream and to think and to wish for himself what he would like to do and to try to follow that path.

AR: I am wondering if your father ever modeled his ambitions for you after the case of the Mozarts where Leopold, who was a musician in his own right, also put this very strong discipline on Wolfgang?

> RS: Well in those days, there was no question that every son, every daughter, had to follow in the footsteps that their parents indicated. The children had absolutely nothing to say about it, and it is possible that my father, who came from Poland, and from the old way of thinking, probably thought he had the right to do that with me, but I don't think he did have the right to do that. He pushed as hard as he possibly could, and he was very well meaning for a while, but when he found out what I did in the way of concerts could lead to a money situation that he liked, I think that he modified his thoughts toward money and that was the bad thing that happened and caused me to run away from home eventually.

AR: In your book you wrote that you played as a child not because of any special gift but because of training, and that goes against the conventional wisdom of people who think that geniuses are born. What do you have to say about that?

> RS: Well, I don't think that geniuses are born, definitely not. I think that a person who has wonderful training as I had had—that's the one thing my father did get for me, he got me the very best training possible—and because of that training I was able to become a pianist and live up to his dream of what I should do. But I think that nobody had to tell him, "Well if you can make money out of this dream its okay," because he certainly did what he could to squeeze whatever he could from my work for his own well being and for the well being of his family.

AR: It is interesting that you mentioned that your father tried to get you the best training possible but at the same time he tried to convey the message that he was the only teacher that you ever had. He was the one who was really behind you as a child pianist. Why do you think he did that?

> **RS:** Well he had a tremendous ego and he probably believed that he was responsible for whatever I did, whether it was playing well, or if I didn't play well he'd beat me until I did play well in his estimation and he didn't believe in giving credit to anybody else. Oh, he asked everybody else to teach me, but he claimed the credit for himself and he was absolutely wrong of course.

AR: One of the things that comes across in your book, *Forbidden Childhood,* is your frankness, your total openness about the story of you and your family. So, I was wondering what led you to write *Forbidden Childhood,* because it must have been very painful for you to write the things that you wrote about your father and your first husband.

> **RS:** Yes, well it was, it was but it's all behind me and a long, long, long time behind me now. My goodness, I have lived three lifetimes since then.

AR: Do you think that it was kind of a liberating experience to write this book?

> **RS:** Well, possibly, possibly. Although, I ran away from home long before the book came, and I think that was the smartest thing I ever did as a youngster was to have the courage to leave home because that home was just crushing me in every way possible.

AR: It is really revealing, and one of the things that you mention in the book, that at an early age you were mystified by the stories of mythical Greeks and Romans. I am wondering whether you think you were attracted to those stories because they were mythological heroes that in a way became independent from established rules and in some way that conveyed to you a message of liberation?

> **RS:** I think so, because I took great joy in anything that was imaginative and those mythological stories, even to this day I like to think back about Perseus and Theseus all of those wonderful Greek mythological characters and Roman mythological characters. Even the story of Pegasus and flying in the sun is a very, very imaginative sort of thing, I like that sort of thing and I like for music to carry people in that way too.

AR: You said in your book that one of the most devastating critiques that you received while becoming a teenager was that the critics were saying that you were playing as an immature person and one wonders, can you teach maturity to a child?

> **RS:** You cannot, and that is where the critics were so stupid. How can you expect from a fourteen or fifteen year old child to play like a mature artist? It is an impossibility because that person is not mature, that person is very young and you cannot complain that a fourteen year old does not play like a thirty-five year old; this is ridiculous.

AR: One of your teachers was Sergei Rachmaninoff and he mentioned to you and your father that you should stop performing in public until the age of 15 in order to become a real artist, a more mature one. Do you think that he was right in that?

RS: I have no idea. That I don't like to comment on because those were the words of a very, very great musician whom I highly respect; I certainly do not want to comment on that, but I think that the one good thing that did come from all the concerts that I played, the only good thing, was that I had the experience of walking on stage. I was not really afraid to walk on stage. So many adults, people with talent, are terribly afraid of walking on stage and performing but I was not because I started so early. That's the only good thing that came of it.

AR: Rachmaninoff was obviously one of the great musicians of the twentieth century. What can you say is the most important memory that you have of him?

RS: That he was a wonderful person, not just a musician! The very first time that I saw him he took from his wallet a picture of a speedboat and I think he loved this speedboat because he kept a picture of it in his wallet. And he said you see this boat, I love this boat, I keep it on a lake in Switzerland and when I am home I go on this boat with my driver and we go all over the lake and go zzzzz all over the lake and we have such a wonderful time. And that kind of calmed me down because I was a little bit afraid of playing for him and he could see that I was shaking. And this got me to laugh and I wasn't shaking anymore, and then he asked me to play. But he was a very wonderful person; in his pocket, he kept little pieces of paper, and on each paper there was a poem cut out from a newspaper or cut out from a magazine. He asked all of his friends to send him these poems, hoping that once he would find a poem and maybe make it into a song, and he very often found inspiration in these poems and he would take one of these poems and he would recite it in his warm Russian way, in Russian, and he would say afterwards, was that not beautiful? And to me of course it was beautiful because he was saying those words but I didn't understand a word of Russian of course.

AR: Rachmaninoff was known for exploring to the limits the expressivity of piano music. How do you determine what the limits of expressivity are, in other words, when do you start deviating from the real intent of the composer?

RS: Well there are no limits. One reason why Rachmaninoff was so great as a teacher is that he did not think like a pianist, he thought like a creative artist because he was a creative artist. I am a re-creative artist, there are many like me who play the music of other people, but Rachmaninoff was from a different kind of artist, he was a creative artist, which meant that he could create music as well as perform it and for him there were no limits and, therefore, he dared to do things that mere pianists don't do and

Ruth leading a piano pedagogy class in her former piano studio at SIUE.
PHOTOGRAPH COURTESY OF PHOTOGRAPHIC SERVICES COLLECTION, UNIVERSITY ARCHIVES, LOVEJOY LIBRARY.

he nudged me in that direction as well, and it was a very wonderful experience. For instance, I played for him one of his own preludes once, and he took me to the window and he said look down at those trees, those are mimosa trees and I want you to play this melody with a golden sound. And I said but how can you make color into a sound on the piano? And I then said the magic words, I said "show me", and he played the first few bars of this prelude and I knew exactly what to do; from there on I was able to do it.

AR: That's a great story. In a way this also reminds me of this famous anecdote when Arturo Toscanini conducted Ravel's *Bolero* and Ravel had figured out that it should last fifteen minutes but Toscanini played much faster and Ravel complained to Toscanini, "why are you performing it so fast, that's not the way I wrote it." And Toscanini replied, "Well, if I had played it the way you wrote it would have been very boring." So I wonder to what extent can you take these kinds of liberties with the original intent of the composer?

RS: Actually it isn't taking a liberty because if you understand a particular sound to be a certain way you cannot mimic that sound, you have to actually create that sound, and in order to create it, maybe you do have to play it a little bit faster or a little bit slower than the composer expected. There are no limits. One of the things that Rachmaninoff taught me is that there is no tempo that is correct for everybody. For me, I would hear a piece that was at a certain tempo and it would be my way of doing it. For another pianist, he would hear it at a different tempo and play it his way. You can take ten great pianists and not two of them would have the same tempo, and this is the way it should be.

AR: In fact you studied with Samuel Barber, one of the most outstanding American composers of the twentieth century, whose "Adagio for Strings" is quite familiar to many people because of its use in the movie, *Platoon;* but when you listen to Barbers' music you feel some kind of tension, some kind of gravity. Since you knew him can you tell this was the product of his own demons, his own conflicts dealing with his own sexuality? What was going on in Barber's mind?

RS: Well first of all I was only five years old when I knew him and he was twenty. He was in the class of Madame Isabelle Vengerova and I was also in the class of Madame Isabelle Vengerova, and it was a class of piano technique. Now in this class there were maybe about ten young people, as I said ranging in age from where I was, age five, to maybe older than twenty, because Barber was not the oldest one in the class. Sam was a wonderful person, and he was particularly wonderful to me because of this story; let me tell you about it. After our class with Madame Vengerova, there was a boy in our class who you all know as Abbey Simon, and he became a famous pianist, and he took me by the hand and he said "do you want to go upstairs and listen to Jorge Bolet's lesson", and so we'd run upstairs and we'd listen outside and we'd hear Jorge Bolet, who has turned into a very great pianist, a specialist in Liszt, and he was having a lesson with his teacher, a Liszt etudes, and we all thought this was fabulous. I would say, "When am I ever going to be able to play a Liszt etudes; I'm just playing a little small piece by Bach, a little small sonata by Mozart, a Liszt etude is just impossible for me." So after a few weeks, Sam Barber noticed that I couldn't wait for the end of the class, I was so eager to go up and listen. He took me by the hand one time and he said Ruth, "I would just like you to understand one thing, you come back listening to Jorge Bolet, listening to short Tchaikovsky play those Liszt etudes, playing those fancy big concertos and he said "you have stars in your eyes and I can see you want to be a pianist like that", and he said "you must not confine yourself to being that kind of a pianist". And I said, "Why not?", and he said "well there are other things to music than playing fast and loud". He said, "people do that to attract attention to themselves, not to the music, and you have to go when you play, you have to see what is inside the music what makes it beautiful". Is it the melody that makes it beautiful? Is it the harmony that makes it beautiful, and if it is the harmony then you must hug your harmony. You must treat music as a very intimate thing, a very precious thing that you have, and you must think of music that way, not in order to attract attention to yourself by playing loud and fast and that was the most important lesson at that time. And I always had a very special feeling for Samuel Barber.

AR: Well no wonder you became also a great teacher because certainly you learned these lessons from the great masters that had such a depth. I am wondering, what was your experience here at Southern Illinois University Edwardsville as a teacher?

RS: Oh I had the honor of teaching so many wonderful young people, so many. Many of them have gone ahead to win prizes with their music, to earn their living through their music. Many of the organists and pianists in the area were my students. I was so amazed when all of them got up and came on stage for a picture, there were more than twenty-five of them in that picture and that was just in a certain period, I had many, many more than those. There are those that have gone ahead, when I went to Korea I found four who had been my students, who are now professors in various universities in Korea. When I went to Australia I found two who had been in my classes at Southern Illinois University who are now teaching in Australia and I had the honor last month only to listen in concert to three people who had been my students.

AR: That's a great reward for you, and I understand that you are still teaching, right?

RS: Yes.

AR: So what drives you to teach at an age when most people feel like retirement is due?

RS: Well, I love music and I love being able to see other people grow a flower just the way I was taught to grow a flower. Maybe Samuel Barber is the person who inspired me there, but his love for music itself was the all encompassing thing, and that is what I try to instill into my students, that music itself is so beautiful and so deserving of attention, and I like to dream of music as being the important thing in people's lives. It is less important in the United States than it is in Asia right now, and that it is in Europe right now. But music is the kind of art that eventually will satisfy more people than any amount of noise, or money or success in any other form. I don't like bombastic movies, I like romantic movies and I think that romance and the beauty of music and that sort of thing will conquer the world eventually.

AR: In your book, *Music at Your Fingertips*, you wrote, "A good teacher will use as many different approaches to instruction as he has students, for two students are not alike." How did you come to the realization that you shouldn't be following a strict method but that this is actually adaptable to different students?

RS: Well, every person is different. Every person's ideas are different. I try to listen to the students' ideas. I try to show them how to follow their particular ideas. No two students have the same ideas about the same piece and when a student tells me, I have an idea how to do this, then I say "Show me, show me, show me. Alright continue this idea, continue, use the pedal over here; it will help. Use these fingers over here; it will help". And in this way I try to get each student to follow his own dream about what the music should say. Not my dream, because my dream belongs to me and his dreams should belong to him, and not have another person impose an idea.

AR: I want to finish with a question that to some people in the audience may sound a little bit macabre, but it is not unusual among musicians, and being the son of a musician myself, I know it is normal talk. The question is, what music would you like to be played at your funeral?

RS: Oh my lord, I'm not even thinking of my funeral (laughter).

AR: Well that shows to you are really still very young at heart and providing a great example to so many people around the world. You are really an outstanding person, and I'm sure that after this interview many more people will want to learn more about you. So do you have a final word for people who want to get into music, for the youngster who wants to get into music?

RS: Well, yes, I would say that the most important thing that you have to do is follow your dream. Follow your dream as far as you can and try to find other people that will help you to follow your dream, because your dream is personal, it is intimate, it's the most important thing that will happen to you, so follow your dream, good luck along the way and believe in yourself. This is very, very important. It may take time before you have other people believing in you but if you believe in yourself and you follow your dream you will have something individual to say, and that's very important.

For Further Reading

"*The Ruth Slenczynska Collection.*" Lovejoy Library, Southern Illinois University Edwardsville. The collection may be accessed at the following Web address: http://www.siue.edu/lovejoylibrary/musiclistening/special_collections/title/slenczynska/slenczynska.shtml .

Slenczynska, R. and L. Biancolli. 1957. *Forbidden Childhood.* NJ: Doubleday & Company, Inc.

Slenczynska, R. and A.M. Lingg. 1961. *Music at Your Fingertips. Aspects of Pianoforte Technique.* London: Herbert Jenkins.

SIUE in the 1970s:
Building a University and *Starting a Career*

by JOE MUNSHAW

The difficulty is that our waking and attentive consciousness scans the world myopically, one thing, one bit, one fragment after another, so that our impressions of life are strung out in a thin scrawny thread, lining up small beads of information; whereas nature itself is a stupendously complex pattern where everything is happening altogether everywhere at once. What we know of it is only what we can laboriously line up and review along the thread of this watchfulness. —ALAN WATTS

Introduction

Last week I was having lunch at Bully's in Edwardsville with two of my favorite SIUE alumni, my sons Mark (B.A. 2008: major in criminal justice, minor in philosophy) and David (B.A. 2009: major in speech communication, minor in sociology). While there I came across an old friend and colleague, Paul Pitts, who was having lunch with Lennox Forrester, the head coach for SIUE men's basketball. There was warmth both in Coach Forrester's voice and handshake, and in his eyes I caught a glimpse of something familiar. Here was a man with a dream and a vision.

In the last few months as I've been writing this chapter, I've found daunting the attempt to communicate the state of this university in the 1970s to the SIUE community in 2011. In my chance meeting with Coach Forrester, it all came into focus. In 2011, Division I basketball program indeed is here. It has personnel and facilities. It has backers and supporters whose dream is to turn it into a winning program. Right now, wins are hard to find. Recognition is elusive. Scoffers and doubters are difficult to refute. The building of the program continues nonetheless.

Such it was with SIUE in the 1970s. We were here: students, faculty, staff, and administration. We had facilities and programs. However, we hadn't done much with it yet. We were mostly potential with little track record. Would we build a university worthy of the students who entered its doors? Would it become a quality institution? Would we be able to attract even better students and faculty? On a personal level, I wondered if I could help build a university to which someday I enthusiastically and proudly would invite my own children to become students.

The Interview

By the time I came to SIUE in 1972 the founding faculty and administrators already had set up the campus and staked out their territories. From 1969 to 1973 they added new tenure track positions and brought in what would be called "The Second Wave" of faculty. In 1972 it was speech communication's turn to hire three new assistant professors.

On a windy, cold, cloudy February day I arrived on campus to interview for one of those positions. Speech Communication was within the Department of Speech and Theatre, within the School of Fine Arts. In those days it worked this way: Hollis White, Dean of Fine

Arts, was a buddy of my mentor at Mizzou, Clifton Cornwell. Dr. Cornwell assured Dean White that I was the best thing to hit academe since Bertrand Russell, and I was as good as hired before I stepped on campus. My day included a walking tour, lunch with speech communication faculty who evidently had no great objections to my hiring, and a half hour meeting with the dean. He offered me a contract on the spot. I would start in September, make $1,100 a month, and hold the rank of Assistant Professor, contingent on completion of my PhD prior to fall quarter. Dean White smiled and said, "I consider myself a benevolent dictator." A semi-radicalized student of the 60s badly in need of a job, I smiled back and thought silently, "We'll see. I think some changes are in order."

Ten days later I called Dean White and said that if he would raise the salary fifty dollars a month, I'd sign. He did...and so did I. Shortly thereafter Dave Valley and Rob Anderson made the same commitment. We became the "three new guys" in speech communication.

The next few months were a whirlwind of completing my active duty assignment in the U.S. Army, finishing and defending my doctoral dissertation, and finding a house. On August 4th I was awarded a PhD by the University of Missouri at Columbia. On August 30th Peter Damien Munshaw changed my name to "Daddy." I had the world by the tail. I was ready to begin my career.

First Day of Classes

In 1972 the core of campus consisted of seven buildings. With much of the university's character and identity to be established in the future, only two buildings then were named after people—Lovejoy Library and Peck Classroom Building. The other buildings were named after their functions: General Office Building (now Rendleman), Science Building, Communications Building (now Dunham Hall), University Center (now Morris University Center). What today is the Spirituality and Sustainability Center was simply the Religious Center. That was it.

I was so excited that I did not sleep the night before classes began. This is a pattern that continued term after term. Eventually I told myself that if I ever lost the excitement and slept soundly the night before a term opens, maybe it would be time to hang it up. Truth be told, I never lost the excitement.

Workers charged with taking care of the buildings and grounds were in a dispute with the university administration, and the day before classes began someone shut off all the air conditioning to campus buildings. I walked into my first class in Peck. It was about 95 degrees in the room and my students were perspiring. They quickly discovered that my syllabus could be used as a fan. I told them to go home, read the syllabus, come back tomorrow, and hopefully things would be better. This was not the way I had envisioned my first day. Later that day the dispute abated, air conditioning was turned on, and we had ourselves a university. It was the only day in my thirty-two years that the university really was not there for its students.

SIUE in the 1970s: A Decade of Healing and Hope

SIUE came to be in a time most turbulent. The Vietnam War divided and disillusioned Americans in so many ways. The assassinations of John F. Kennedy, Martin Luther King, Jr., and Bobby Kennedy left people stunned, sad, angry and numb. The civil rights actions, marches and protests, and the resulting landmark voting rights and public accommodations legislation brought change with a steep price. A U.S. president resigned in disgrace. Trust in authority of all types diminished. Strife left deep wounds, while the beneficial changes brought forth hardly had begun to bear fruit.

A university is both an idea and a place that invites students to enter with their hopes and dreams. The basic promise is that this is where one can build a foundation that will make those dreams become reality. In the 1970s SIUE had not yet established a track record of making dreams come true. We had a few alumni, but most of them were just getting started in their careers. Many of our students were the first in their families to pursue higher education.

Often our students lacked the wherewithal to go to college elsewhere, and SIUE had become their choice by default. Nonetheless, the daughters and sons in southern Illinois had a new option for getting a university education. Who knew then what they would become? Who knew what SIUE would become?

In my classes were sisters, brothers, widows and friends of young men killed in Vietnam. There were Vietnam veterans who were back home in a nation that certainly was not thanking them for their service. A few had visible wounds. Many more suffered from PTSD, the effects of Agent Orange, and things we didn't even have words or concepts for yet.

In the early 1970s there were few, if any, students on campus who called themselves African Americans. There were negroes, blacks, Blacks, Afro Americans, Afro-Americans. Racial labels and identities were in transition. Black Power, Black Pride, and militancy were in ascendency. The "N-word" euphemism was not yet coined, and its nasty, harsh and degrading predecessor had not yet been excised from the minds, hearts, and sometimes the lips of many on campus. The doors were open, yet many barriers remained. Would SIUE become a place where promises of the civil rights movement might be fulfilled? In the 1970s this remained an open question.

I recall a class discussion in which a couple of black students talked about being followed around in stores simply because of the color of their skin and the presumption that they were shoplifters. I expressed some skepticism, and one of my students challenged me to go into the local K-Mart and watch what happened when she shopped. "OK," I said, "let's see." I kept my distance from her when I arrived at K-Mart. She got a shopping cart, and began to place items in it. Within five minutes a store employee began to shadow her every move. She wandered through the store and had about fifteen items in her cart. Eventually she turned to the employee and said, "Experiment is over. You can go ahead and put these items back on the shelves." My students taught me to see some barriers to which I had been blind.

Building a Speech Communication Curriculum

The entire tenure-track speech communication faculty in 1972 had earned degrees in rhetoric and public address. Most had written doctoral dissertations on some aspect of political rhetoric. The curriculum, which was inherited from our association with Carbondale, emphasized platform speaking, debate, persuasion, and rhetorical theory. The required general education freshman course in speech was a public speaking course entitled "Oral Communication of Ideas."

Part of the excitement of being at a university without an established identity was that there were few entrenched traditions, and the possibilities for innovation and experimentation were expansive. In my academic field the whole area of interpersonal communication was just beginning. It wasn't even established yet whether the word "interpersonal" should have a hyphen in it. As a graduate student I had taught from the first published interpersonal communication textbook in our undergraduate basic course.

In a culture where families, communities, and familiar associations had been fractured by the upheaval of the 1960s, there was more demand for communication competence in the private sphere than in the public. To be an effective orator or platform speaker took on less value than being an effective listener and negotiator in the nitty-gritty of daily life. In a time when so many people were divided by walls, the need was for bridge builders. In fact, one of the first interpersonal communication textbooks adopted at SIUE was John Stewart's *Bridges Not Walls*.

We transformed the basic speech course into an interpersonal communication skills course, and added an advanced course in the area because student response to the basic course was so positive. We added an advanced organizational communication course, which addressed the importance of interpersonal communication skills among professionals in organizational settings. Our communication theory course moved away from narrow treatments of communication as rhetoric, and opened up the plethora of new communication theories that had come into academe in the post-World War II period. A listening course and family communication course were added to the curriculum. Annette Graebe developed a course in public relations and began a chapter of the Public Relations Student Association on campus. Not long after that we added a second public relations course.

The Interracial Communication Course

In the mid-1970s the departmental faculty encouraged Dave Valley and me to develop an experimental course in interracial communication with specific focus on communication between whites and blacks in American society. There were no textbooks in interracial communication. As best we could determine there were no such courses in other colleges and universities. Our speech communication faculty was entirely white, and at the time we did not yet have any black graduate students who were teaching assistants. Additionally, we had not established a network of African American speech communication colleagues in other institutions. We were not starting from a position of strength, but our perceived need for a course of this kind compelled us to proceed.

We decided that the interracial communication course would work best in an intensive workshop format, should emphasize communication exercises and experiences over theory, and should have roughly equal numbers of white and black students. We would not exclude international students or students with Hispanic or Asian backgrounds from the course, but the course focus still would be on communication between blacks and whites in American society with special emphasis on interracial communication at SIUE.

The course filled quickly when enrollment opened. I taught it the first time. Most students were skeptical that one course could do much to improve what we then called "race relations" on campus, but any attempt to do so seemed better than nothing. We met eight hours a day for five days. Students brought lifetimes of experiences, many of them frustrating, to the classroom. Grievances galore abounded. Given the format of the course, it became clear that there would be time for everyone to be heard. It was a challenge to keep interruptions to a minimum. It was an emotional class. Much anger, shouting, defensiveness, crying, quite a bit of laughter, even awe and silence in response to students' stories. Students heard things they were uncomfortable hearing. Students found themselves challenged on their generalizations and stereotypes. Nobody dropped the class. Most students became bonded in ways that surprised them. I remember one student the last day saying something to the effect that "this country is messed up, man, and so is this campus, but you guys are OK." A strong sentiment in course reviews was that "everybody should be required to take this course." I was exhausted at the end of the workshop. I remember going to hear Bob Dylan at the Muny (an outdoors theater facility in St. Louis) that Friday night and hearing his music through a whole new filter that the workshop provided.

Over time the interracial communication course got better and stronger. Utilizing student feedback and finding exercises that worked or didn't work, the format evolved. Rudy Wilson, SIUE's then Assistant Provost for Cultural and Social Diversity, generously offered to work with us in team teaching the course, and we moved to the team teaching format that is still in place today. Research progressed in the area of interracial communication and textbooks were written. Something good got started at SIUE, and it is gratifying to have been a part of it.

SIUE President John S. Rendleman

The university administration was housed in the General Office Building, which we often called "The Hill." When I came to SIUE, the man on top of The Hill was John Rendleman. He was a short man with a larger than life personality. The administration he ran was not particularly open or transparent, but his door was open and once he met someone, he remembered his/her name.

He was a great encourager of new faculty. Our performance was critical to the strong and vibrant university he dreamed of building. In my third year I received an excellence award for young teachers from the Central States Speech Association. The letter of congratulations he sent me contained a sentence that I've held in my mind and heart for decades: "…those of us who have been watching you are not the least bit surprised, now keep up the good work." I would have walked through a brick wall for the man.

President Rendleman believed that if SIUE was to become known and respected that he had to get people on campus, to experience the farmland that had been turned into a university. A top priority was funding for music and performing arts. On the music faculty were world class concert pianist Ruth Slenzynska Kerr, John Kendall, who developed the Suzuki Program for teaching violin to youngsters which gained national recognition, and Leonard Van Camp, who grew the University Chorale into an organization which went on to compete in and win regional, national, and international music competitions.

The Mississippi River Festival (MRF) became a phenomenon that brought hundreds of thousands of people to campus. A large open tent at the bottom of a gently sloping hill provided an outdoor performing arts venue that could accommodate more than 30,000 people. Lawn seat tickets were $2.50 in the early 70s. MRF booked top recording artists and celebrities, and people came. The St. Louis Symphony Orchestra would give one or two concerts each summer. Decades later when I meet some people and tell them about SIUE, they eagerly share experiences they had at MRF concerts.

Streaking, running nude in public, was a fad that came to campus on at least two occasions in the 1970s. Word was out one warm, spring day that there was going to be a streaking on campus, and hundreds of the campus community were in the quadrangle when a dozen or so students streaked from behind the University Center to behind the Science Building where cars were waiting to pick them up. The local press converged on John Rendleman's office, demanding to know

Scene from the Mississippi River Festival.
PHOTOGRAPH COURTESY OF PHOTOGRAPHIC SERVICES COLLECTION, UNIVERSITY ARCHIVES, LOVEJOY LIBRARY.

what he intended to do about the streaking. He responded that he thought he just might get himself a more powerful set of binoculars. This provided a laugh, a quote for the news, and the journalists were on their way. Streaking ended rapidly enough on its own.

John Rendleman died of cancer at age forty eight on March 4, 1976. Without his vision and commitment MRF lasted only a few more years. However, SIUE fared much better. He helped us expand on the idea that this university was here, it was doing good things, and it was going places. The university honored itself in naming the administration building after Rendleman; he was such a key player in giving SIUE an identity and encouraging staff, faculty and students to really make something of this place.

Springfest 1975

When I buy potatoes for cooking, I usually store them in a paper bag and put them in a cool, dark place in my basement. They keep well for a long time that way. However, if left in the dark long enough, potatoes will shrivel and sprout. In the spring of 1975 when cleaning out my basement, I discovered two or three gnarly looking potatoes with five- or six-inch sprouts all over them. This I saw as an opportunity. I picked out the strangest looking one, put it in a shoebox and poked nine or ten holes in the box.

I took the potato to campus and brought it to class—"Take Your Potato To Work Day." I told my students I had a pet in the box and that if they would be very quiet, I'd let them see it. They gathered around the desk, shoulder to shoulder in anticipation. Then I opened the lid and threw the potato into the crowd. Shrieks, squeals, and lots of laughter. For the remainder of the class period I would hold and pet the potato. It was a great way to keep students' attention, although I'm sure that some of them were glad that they were between the door and me.

Springfest as an institution was just getting started. It included several bands, eats and treats, tricycle races, and a frog-jumping contest. I decided to pay the ten-cent fee and enter my potato in the frog-jumping contest. My department chair had a bullwhip hanging from a bookshelf in his office. I think he considered it some kind of leadership metaphor. I asked to borrow the bullwhip and put it in the shoebox with the potato. Only one other person, a student, had entrants in the frog-jumping contest; he had two frogs. Before the start he asked if he could see my frog. I declined, saying that my frog was a highly trained athlete, and he presently was meditating prior to the jump.

My potato/frog drew first jump, and I put it on the starting line and started cracking the bullwhip over it. The student with the two frogs wanted me to be disqualified. The judges just looked at the potato and said nothing. As you might guess, the potato just sat there; it didn't jump forward (or backward). The student put his two frogs through their paces. One jumped about ten inches forward. The other jumped about ten inches backward. So my potato finished second in the contest. I was pretty proud of it.

SIUE has gone on to have bigger and better Springfests through the years. It now has a magnificent sculpture to mark the arrival of spring equinox. There was a time, however, when not only a live cougar, but also a potato roamed the campus in spring.

Concluding Thought

I continued teaching at SIUE for another twenty five years after the 1970s concluded. The number of buildings in the core of campus nearly doubled. The faculty and administration became much more diverse. Policies designed to promote equity, diversity, and safety were written and revised. As SIUE's identity became clearer, the university community came together to explicitly develop and communicate a vision and core values. In the 1970s we were much more flying by the seat of our pants. Good people, good times, good work.

For Further Reading

Godwin, Robert. *One Cosmos Under God.* Paragon House, 2004.
  ISBN 1-55778-836-7

Joynes, Monty. *Naked Into the Night.* Hampton Roads Publishing, 1997.
  ISBN 978-1571740557

Wilber, Ken. *Kosmic Consciousness.* Sounds True, 2005. This is a CD set of a twelve-hour interview with Ken Wilber. He provides an excellent overview of his philosophy and work. ASIN B000Q25R04

Zink, Nelson. *The Structure of Delight.* Nightway Press, 1991, 1998.
  ISBN 0-9665325-0-3

Accidental Achievement

by MARIAN SMITH

January 1979:
For 15 years, my children and I had followed my husband through the oilfields of the US, South America, North Africa and the UK. We were in Scotland when two of Aberdeen's finest arrived at my door to tell me that my husband had died of a coronary in Heathrow Airport. My teenage son and I left Scotland and returned to Oklahoma to join my daughter, who was in her second semester at Southwestern Oklahoma State University in Weatherford. When we arrived, she said, "Mom, living in the states will be an adjustment for you." She was right.

The kids were in school, and I drove around a lot. At 38, I was too young to retire and possibly too old to do much. Sitting alone in a truck stop café on I40 in Central Oklahoma, less than 100 miles from where I was born, I ignored my plate of ham and eggs and glanced around at the people in the restaurant. The waitress was a pro, carrying three plates of food in each hand, moving rapidly between tables and kitchen. She spoke to the cook in a code I'd never learned, and she looked tired. "No, that's not for me," I mumbled to myself, "I don't speak the language and I can't handle more than one plate without spilling, besides, I already feel tired." Observations in the mall, in a junior high classroom, and a part-time stint as a receptionist for the local undertaker gave me a similar disinclination to embark on those careers. My best memories of the mortuary were the jokes: A pallbearer asked the funeral director to help him with his tie. The mortician said, "Certainly, lie down."

Still, I had to do something within reason, and preferably something I considered worth doing. Many things were beyond either my age or ability: I didn't have the manual skills required of a surgeon or a dentist, the patience to teach in the public schools, or the smooth tongue required to become a sales person; all useful occupations, if not plausible for me. I had no talent in the arts and I had no interest in manual labor. One day, on my way back to Oklahoma after a trip to the Canadian Rockies, I gazed up at the glittering angel Moroni trumpeting the arrival of heavenly knowledge to Salt Lake City believers, and thought of something that I had done proficiently twenty years earlier. I had been a good student, and I thought that the judgment that comes with maturity and experience would compensate for any decline in short-term memory. I could see no reason not to pursue a degree or two. At the least I would occupy my time and do something potentially useful.

June 1979:
I loved the little town of Weatherford, and the familiar atmosphere of a college classroom. Because my daughter was at Southwestern, I began my new academic life there. I chose a summer course in optics, because it sounded like fun. I sat in a front-row seat, smiling and nodding in agreement with the professor who assured us that the properties of light were fascinating, and that we would love the course. Certainly I would, I thought, I loved to learn and file away

facts of most every kind. It sounded as interesting as a talk at the British Museum or a tour through Westminster Abbey. Fifteen minutes later I glanced around the room and discovered that, unlike the visitors to museums and churches, this audience was taking notes. They knew we would be tested on some of these shiny properties, and I belatedly remembered that students received grades. Although I didn't know it at the time, I had begun the educational phase that was to shape the rest of my life.

Although I had completed the BS degree in mathematics in 1962, I knew I was not a mathematician, and had no interest in taking another math course. My undergraduate minor was biology (a total of four courses), and Southwestern offered a MEd in that subject. Although I had no intention of teaching, I took the required 8 hours of education and enrolled in courses in botany, a subject that I considered intellectually interesting, with the enormous benefit that there would be no distressing animal dissection, which would have disrupted my comfort zone. Among the eight biology faculty were two great botanists, an extraordinary occurrence in a department so small, both of whom were my age. Dr. Segal, a University of Kansas PhD, was small and dark, with a perpetual air of cynicism and a reputation as a taskmaster. He was, in fact, a softhearted man and a great teacher. He and his wife had a small farm near town and their living room featured 8x10 portraits of their four Alpine goats. The other botanist, Dr. Seibert, who completed his PhD at North Carolina State, appeared to be jolly, informal in his approach to education, and friendly. His cynicism was hidden behind a rather frenetic jocular bonhomie and his classes were as exciting as walking through a minefield. His supporters, students who loved his edgy brilliance and valued his knowledge, trekked around the Southwest with him in a van, learning to appreciate the variety of plants and their tenacity in adapting to every landscape. They also learned to survive the quixotic decisions Dr. Seibert made about where to pitch our tents and build our campfire. My most vivid memory of one such trip was camping at 10,000 ft in the Rocky Mountains. It was early spring and bitterly cold. During the night, the wind roared over our tents like a frozen dervish and deposited the wet canvas on top of us. I was forty years old, already a bit too stiff to sleep comfortably on the ground, and believed that camping out meant staying in The Hilton. In spite of that, I loved Weatherford and I thrived at Southwestern.

After three years in Weatherford, Dr. Segal began campaigning for me to apply to the KU graduate program in botany, and Dr. Seibert was equally determined for me to pursue graduate work at NC State. Both schools had outstanding botany programs. I, however, liked to ski, and neither North Carolina nor Kansas could lay claim to much in the way of ski slopes, so I applied to the state universities in Wyoming and Montana and drove up to check them (and their ski areas) out. They all appeared to want me, but their botany programs were miniscule, and they couldn't guarantee graduate assistant support. This made me nervous. After all, I'd escaped the uncertainties of the international oilfields and now I wanted a few guarantees to make me feel secure. So, I applied to KU and NC State, hoping for more solid support.

March 1982:
The Southwestern Lady Bulldog basketball team was on their way to Kansas City to play in the NAIA final four, and I decided to drive up and give them my vocal and moral support. When Dr. Segal found out that I was to be less than 30 miles from Lawrence and KU, he encouraged me to visit the campus and talk to the faculty in the Department of Botany. On my way home from a disappointing final round in which the Lady Bulldogs had been deprived of their much deserved championship, I stopped by KU. To my surprise, I was greeted and interviewed by a child prodigy (or so he seemed to me) named Dr. Craig Martin, who had wild curly red hair and a beard any Scot would be proud of. Within the hour, he had spoken with the chair of the Botany Department and offered me graduate support if I would become his first PhD student. Craig, it turned out, was 26 years old (16 years my junior), a graduate of Duke, and in his second

year at KU. I told him that because I would be nudging 50 by the time I graduated, I worried about getting a job with my shiny new PhD, and, therefore, would like to complete the degree in three years. Did he think that possible? He said, "I don't know, but we can certainly try."

Craig is a plant ecological physiologist, and I thought, "As soon as I find out what that is, I'll learn to be one too." To say that Craig is unusual is not sufficient. He is a brilliant young man who became my mentor and constant companion for the next three and a half years. He lived in a tiny three-room house where he had riotous dinner parties at which he served no meat, but plenty of beer.

The Botany Department at KU was small and there was considerable socializing between and among graduate students and faculty. This was particularly beneficial to me because otherwise I might have felt alienated from others in the program because of my age and lack of previous research expertise. We had theme parties, went to Jayhawk basketball games, celebrated Christmas with a dinner of roast goose and gift exchanges, and provided support for any student who was facing prelim or oral exams. Group membership changed with graduations and job offers. Craig and I went to the movies, and when we saw Conan the Barbarian, Craig shouted out, "Uhh, Conan" at moments he considered pertinent to the film. He traveled with me over the whole of Kansas to do my fieldwork. In the grocery store, he repeatedly pushed his goods back before they arrived at the point where the rubber conveyer belt disappeared to circle again, patiently explaining to the clerk that otherwise they'd keep on going and fall off the end of the checkout counter. During the time I was at KU, I never saw Craig break into a smile during one of these performances. His deadpan delivery conveyed an air of gravity that must have baffled a legion of clerks.

In my final year at KU, I was hospitalized with a severe stomach ulcer attack (small wonder) and Craig smuggled a ½ pint of whiskey and a *Playboy* magazine into my room, glancing behind him in a parody of a spy in enemy territory. After my door was safely closed, he read the magazine and drank the whiskey. He was a great teacher and an outstanding scholar who could make significant progress on writing a paper in a 15-minute break. When I wasn't along to entertain him, he claimed he wrote some of his best papers while driving. Only once did I know of this to backfire: He came to a T-junction in rural Kansas and drove straight through, stranding his car in the ditch. I loved KU; the botany students who offered unstinting support for a woman who had spent most of her adult life as a housewife and was at least ten-years their senior, and Craig. It would be difficult to overstate Craig's influence on my life and on my ability to deal with the difficult or unexpected. He taught me how to look for and seize every opportunity to advance my career and he gave me great advice: If a physiologist asks you a question, plead ignorance on the basis that you're an *ecologist*, if an ecologist asks a question you can't answer, tell him you're a *physiologist*.

He taught me everything I know about plant ecological physiology, and more importantly, how to build a research program on a shoestring. Other graduate students saw their mentors occasionally; but because I was his only graduate student, I saw Craig almost daily, through trauma (his and mine) and success. If I had been in a large lab with an uninvolved mentor, I doubt that I would have become the academic that I did. I had inadvertently chosen the perfect person with whom to complete my graduate work. Ultimately, I had to leave the nest. I applied for jobs, and Craig drove me to the airport, dispensing advice on how to behave during an interview, "Check out the faculty and show an interest in talking with them about their disciplines, know what courses are taught in the department and be specific about how you might strengthen their curriculum, ask questions about research opportunities in the department and describe some potential projects that you could successfully complete under prevailing departmental conditions."

Craig and I pose following hooding ceremony at KU in 1986.
PHOTOGRAPH BY SARA LASLEY.

June 1986:
I received one solid job offer, so I left for Spearfish, South Dakota to become an assistant professor of biology. I loved Spearfish, the spectacular Black Hills, the friendly people who welcomed me as one of their own, and some of the best students I ever had the joy to teach. Unfortunately, the only skiing I got to do was cross-county, at which I was terrible, and it wore me out. It seemed to me that I taught most everything in the College of Sciences: basic biology, biology for elementary and secondary education majors, botany, plant physiology, college algebra, and worst of all, business math. The only time in my 23-year teaching career that I completely forgot to attend a class was the one in business math when I was supposed to teach the students about amortization on a loan. One cold February afternoon during the second semester, I was sitting in my office considering Black Hills State University and Spearfish. I loved them both, but how on earth was I going to hold up to 17 contact hours per week in the classroom,

successfully teach a double lab in basic biology (the wall between two labs had been removed so that the hapless teacher, working at the demonstration desk in the center, stood to the side of the table so that the 30 students in each room could see what was happening), and establish some kind of research program without a dedicated lab space?

The phone rang. "Hello, Dr. Smith?"

"Yes, this is she."

A short pause and then the sound of a clearing throat, "This is Dr. Brugam. I'm chair of the hiring committee for the biology position for which you interviewed last year at SIUE, but, ahem, uhm, it's a little embarrassing to admit, but we couldn't make up our mind who to hire, uh, then. Would you be willing to come see us again and, uh, interview for the position in biology that we discussed before?"

"Does the position still require no more than two courses and a seminar per semester, as long as I'm willing to build an externally funded research program?" I breathlessly inquired. What I didn't ask was whether I would ever be required to teach business math again, or to face a double lab with 60 students, but these demands were very unlikely, after all, SIUE had a well-staffed math department and I'd seen their teaching labs, all were too small to hold more than 25 students.

"Yes," said Dr. Brugam, and I knew all I needed to know about the new direction my academic career was going to take. After all, as embarrassed as he was about one hesitation on their part, I doubted that they would turn me down again. We were all friendly and collegial, and I aimed my Mazda RX-7 toward southern Illinois as soon as the summer semester at Black Hills State ended.

August 1987:
Dr. Baich, then the chair of the Biology Department, offered me her basement apartment to bunk in until I was able to locate a place to live in Edwardsville. I arranged for a property manager to show me what was available to rent or lease. I dragged myself from one dismal apartment, with carpet that smelled of too much partying gone wild (Reefer Madness?), to a tiny condo that had walls so thin I could hear

Lab group gathered outside the Science Building for our semester photo portrait. To Marian's right stand six graduate and six undergraduate students who completed *Boltonia* projects during their time at SIUE.

PHOTOGRAPH BY DR. NANCY PARKER.

and clearly understand a conversation taking place in an adjoining unit. I said, "I can't live here, I have a piano, which I like to play. Even if my neighbors don't drive me crazy, my plunking would cause them to revolt." After about a half-dozen such accommodations, just as I feared that I'd be commuting from St. Louis, my helpful guide said, "Would you like a *nice* place?"

Duh! "Well, yes, please" I said with remarkable restraint, considering that I had a smashing headache by that time.

He took me to a two-bedroom house on Franklin Avenue that was perfect: Plenty of room for my piano, no attached noisy neighbors, and a remodeled kitchen. I loved it. I can only assume I had appeared to be too poor to afford a nice place. Is this what people always think of university professors? With a new job and home secured, I left my RX-7 parked in Dr. Baich's driveway and flew back to Spearfish to supervise the removal of my household goods and to drive my nearly new 4-wheel drive Bronco, bought the previous October 1st when we had our first snowstorm, to Edwardsville.

Before the semester began, Dr. Baich told me that she had planned to give me a free semester that fall, so I could organize my research lab; however, the faculty member who had been scheduled to teach the introductory non-majors biology course had become ill and would be on leave for the semester. I would have a total of three contact hours per week and be assigned a teaching assistant who would keep my roll and grade my papers. Magnanimously, I assured her I was up to the challenge (remember the 17 contact hours and business math at my last job?). I got off to a great start: The teaching was rewarding and the campus was heaven for a botanist. I'd be able to conduct many of my labs in our prairie, or forest, or along the ravines. I also realized that even if I never secured any funding, I could complete any number of interesting and publishable research projects without leaving campus. Every day during every season, I walked the trails and ravines of the campus and discovered a treasury of native plants. I eventually bought a house within a block of the bike path. Then I bought a bike, so I could ride to school each day. I attracted my first two graduate students, and we published work within the first two years of my SIUE career. I settled in my new house and grew more confident in my position at SIUE.

At the beginning of my second semester at SIUE, I began to acquire the equipment I would need for classes and research. A plant growth chamber was a necessity, so I wrote a small NSF Instrumentation grant, and it was funded. After I received the news, Dr. Myer, the Dean of the School of Sciences, rewarded me with a cutting edge system to measure photosynthesis. I was in heaven. A little success and a heightened presence brought more students to study in the lab and wonderful financial support from the Graduate School. I loved the Grad School, and with good reason: They supported my research from the beginning with a variety of small awards and became my willing accomplices in taking care of the nuts and bolts of administering my external grant money. I applied for early tenure and promotion on the strength of a second NSF research grant and my new publications. Life was good; SIUE was the perfect place, and I had arrived here at the perfect time.

During my first year at SIUE, my lab group was small, but enthusiastic. The students decorated the door to the lab (unheard of in our department in those days), and marched in the Edwardsville Halloween parade pulling our little Red Flyer full of plants from the greenhouse sporting a banner that said, "SIUE Botany Department." Like Jack's beanstalk, my lab grew and grew. My students and I gave presentations at every opportunity to share our work and an amazing number of graduate and undergraduate students wanted to join us. This was great, but I needed to find worthwhile projects for them all and the financial means to support them and our work.

May 1991:
The phone rang. "Hello, Dr. Smith?"

"This is she."

"My name is Tom Keevin, and I am the St. Louis district biologist for the US Army Corps of Engineers. One of your colleagues told me that you are a botanist and might be interested in doing a project for us on a threatened species, *Boltonia decurrens,* a plant that grows only in the floodplain of the Illinois River Valley."

Sitting up straight in my office chair and coming to professional attention, I said, "Absolutely. When do we start?" Thus began a 15-year project that provided funding and thesis projects for 50 graduate students and a larger number of undergraduates. Although the Corps project was limited to two years of funding, The Great Flood of 1993 turned this modest beginning into a tidal wave (pardon the pun) of money and opportunity. In 1995, I was swept along by the floodwaters to a 5-year NSF grant that ensured my promotion to full professor and enabled me to attract additional funding from other agencies. The result was that I ran a 15-person lab for 10 years, supported students financially, helped them complete research-based degrees, took them to regional and national meetings where they presented

Marian collecting seeds in Mason County, IL in 2010 for the Center for Plant Conservation seed bank at the Missouri Botanical Garden.

PHOTOGRAPH BY DR. NANCY PARKER.

their research, and provided sufficient data for me to retire in 2008 with a respectable list publications and the rank of Distinguished Professor of Research in Biology.

We had a great time doing all of this. My work attracted a wide variety of students. Many of the conservation activists in the department joined us, virtually all of the vegetarians chose our lab (a bit of a puzzle to me), and because I worked to explain the ecology, physiology and demography of *Boltonia,* students from our environmental studies MS program found a niche analyzing the chemical makeup of the floodplain habitat and *Boltonia's* response to environmental pollution. We met once a week for an hour (an absolute requirement for staying in the lab) to share our various progress reports, to request field or lab help when necessary, to discuss arrangements for upcoming trips, and to eat. We became famous for the number of papers we presented at state and national meetings and my students' presence *en masse* in support of their lab mates when they presented a conference paper or a thesis defense. We took turns bringing lunch for everyone in the lab at the weekly meetings and celebrated each holiday by eating and laughing our way through it.

I enjoyed teaching and found that an interesting class was the most effective way to attract students to our lab. I experimented with co-operative learning, group and individual research projects, online quizzes, and rewarding students in my non-majors introductory biology course points for good attendance. And always, I took students out on our campus at every opportunity. Both graduate and undergraduate students became co-authors on my publications. When senior projects became a requirement in our department, we were ahead of the curve. My undergraduate students already had research projects in progress and they knew how to present them orally or by poster. Long before there was a large format printer in the department, we had our posters printed in color and laminated at Kinko's. I was proud to be associated with my students and could not have built a research program without them. Teaching and research merged to coalesce all of the stops and starts in my erratic post-40 life into a meaningful crescendo that was more exciting and rewarding than I could ever have imagined.

March 2011:
I have been retired now for nearly three years and am still amazed that each accidental turn in my life placed me in the right place at the right time and in the company of the right people. The contacts I made while at SIUE have proven valuable in my retirement. I continue to work with conservation and agency personnel on rare and endangered plant species, which allows me to continue my fieldwork and to publish my research. The US Fish &Wildlife Agency honored me as the "Endangered Species Recovery Champion of 2010," and I received the award at a ceremony in Kansas City in March 2011. Maybe it is true that there are no accidents, just opportunities. If so, I've had more than my share of both.

For Further Reading

Changnon, Stanley A. 1996. *The Great Flood of 1993.* Westview Press, Inc.

Middleton, Beth. 1999. *Wetland restoration.* John Wylie & Sons, Inc.

Smith, Marian and Paige Mettler. 2002. The flood pulse and *Boltonia decurrens.* Chapter 4, In: *Flood pulsing in the wetlands* (ed. Beth Middleton). John Wylie & Sons.

Smith, Marian, Hal Caswell and Paige Mettler-Cherry 2005. Stochastic flood and precipitation regimes and the population dynamics of a threatened floodplain plant. *Ecological Applications,* 15(3): 1036-1052.

Wilson, E. O. 1999. *The Diversity of Life.* W.W. Norton & Co.

LEADERSHIP and Culture: Overcoming Challenges and Building a Future

by DAVID SILL

As a child, I had two uncles who worked at small colleges, one a professor of history at Linfield College in McMinnville, Oregon, and the other the Dean of George Williams College in Downers Grove, Illinois. I remember going to the campuses, hearing the stories, and learning of my uncles' work. The work my uncles did was consequential—their work made a difference. From a very early age, I thought that perhaps, perhaps I might follow them into academe.

Coming of age during the 1960's, I grew up in Walnut Creek, California, about 20 miles from Berkeley. During high school, my friends and I would go to Telegraph Avenue with its used bookstores such as Moe's and its odd assortment of street people. We would go to local coffee shops with their beatnik persona, poetry readings, and jazz bands, and we would go to the other cultural and political resources surrounding the University of California. We would go to Sproul Plaza and Sather Gate on the Cal campus with its soapbox evangelists, pick up conga drum bands, and kids swimming in the fountain. I never intended to go to Berkeley for college, though I did end up there during 1968 to avoid the draft. That year was a year of civil strife—urban riots, anti-war demonstrations, the Black Panthers, Martin Luther King's assassination and Bobby Kennedy's. Thinking back to the attitudes and values that have guided me through the years, I believe the year spent in Berkeley in 1968 was formative in ways that I was unaware of at the time.

After finally beating the draft by spending four years in the Air Force, I graduated from the University of California at Berkeley in 1973. I completed my graduate work at Michigan State University in 1979 and got my first faculty appointment at a small Catholic college in Cincinnati named Edgecliff College. It was run by the Sisters of Mercy.

Edgecliff College was a good little school, with 900 students on a campus overlooking the Ohio River. The pay was not much, and with a family of three we were not going to get rich. But there were compensating benefits that came with working at a good small college that provided at least some compensation for the low salary. The faculty was collegial, caring, and committed to student success. The students wanted to be there, brought a good learning attitude with them, and were willing to work. My office was on the second floor of a renovated 19th century mansion with large windows that overlooked the Ohio River. And my classroom was across the hall. There was much that was good about that first year at Edgecliff College.

Edgecliff Corbett Theater offices and lobby, 1989.
PHOTOGRAPH BY DOROTHY SILL.

Unfortunately, by Thanksgiving, things started to fall apart. We started hearing rumors about fiscal problems. The Sisters of Mercy who ran the college were losing money and looking for a way to get out from the fiscal strains of running a small college under fiscal duress. Right before Thanksgiving break, the Dean announced that talks had begun with Xavier University for some kind of cooperative program. Xavier is a Jesuit institution a few miles down the road from Edgecliff College, and rumors started that Edgecliff and Xavier were going to merge. These rumors were reinforced right before Christmas break when another announcement came out that merger was being considered.

As the year progressed, the faculty had hopes that their salaries might increase if there were a merger with Xavier because Xavier faculty earned two to three times what Edgecliff faculty earned. At the same time, there were fears that the advantages of being at a small college, the unique nature of the programs and the students, and the sense of community would disappear—the very reasons that most of the faculty had chosen to be there. As we approached the end of the academic year, it appeared that Edgecliff College was going to become Edgecliff College of Xavier University under control of the Jesuits, but there were no specific details.

We were told that Xavier wanted Edgecliff College because of the strength of its arts programs, programs that Xavier did not have. The Edgecliff College theater program had a long history of excellence and housed the first professional repertory theater company in Cincinnati. There are parallels to the St. Louis Repertory Theater that started at Webster College and continues on the Webster University campus today. While the repertory theater moved off the Edgecliff College campus to become Cincinnati Playhouse in the Park, the Edgecliff theater program remained strong. There was no theater program at Xavier, no department, and only one theater faculty member. The art department at Edgecliff also had an extremely strong faculty, with a

Overlook of the Ohio River from Edgecliff College Campus, outside the Art Building. David Sill and father, C. E. Sill, 1989.

PHOTOGRAPH BY DOROTHY SILL.

good reputation, and excellent facilities. The idea that the strength of the arts programs explained why the Jesuits wanted Edgecliff College made some sense, at least to those of us in the arts, but the cynics on the faculty argued that the Jesuits only really wanted the real estate with its prime location on the bluffs overlooking the Ohio River within three miles of downtown Cincinnati.

In the end, we got answers to what was going to happen the day before commencement in May. Every faculty member was called in to talk individually with the Xavier Provost. That was the day we learned that the entire theatre and art faculty was pink slipped. In fact, the entire Edgecliff College faculty was fired. Edgecliff College was shut down, and Xavier University was going to start an Edgecliff College of Xavier University with the Edgecliff students and on the Edgecliff campus. But the existing college was closed. This voided tenure contracts. Xavier wanted the students and the facilities but not the faculty.

After learning what happened to the faculty, the students organized a demonstration, organized a press briefing for the local media, and made public something that Xavier had wanted to keep private and quiet. What Xavier had not counted on was that many of the theater students were working the day before commencement on reorganizing prop storage. The students were there on campus when the Xavier Provost notified the Edgecliff College faculty that they would not be retained, and tenure be damned. If we had not hired the students to work that day, they would have already left campus and would not have been there to organize their demonstration. Their demonstration made the evening news and a story on the front page of the morning newspaper. With my background at Berkeley, the ability of the Edgecliff students to organize an effective demonstration on very short notice made me proud.

Xavier offered the faculty one year of salary as severance pay, which dropped to 10% if we got a new job. At this point, many of us were thinking job and paycheck, not faculty career. So I started to look. Fortunately for me, Southern Illinois University Edwardsville was searching for an entry- level faculty position that matched my background perfectly. And SIUE was searching for the position in the summer because the department did not have travel funding for bringing in candidates for interviews until the new fiscal year started on July 1. In the end, I got the job starting Fall 1980. My coming to SIUE was entirely unplanned and at the time was just a job.

During the summer before moving to Edwardsville, I designed and served as technical director for a production of *The Sound of Music* at the Edgecliff summer theater. At the end of the summer theater season, Xavier offered me a position to manage the Edgecliff theater facility for them. I remember listening to the offer from the Xavier theater faculty member who had come to talk with me. We were sitting on a stone wall at the back of the scene shop. I said that I had already gotten another job on the faculty at SIUE. He asked what I was going to earn. When I told him that SIUE was going to pay me over 70% more than what I had been earning, his only response was, "Oh." And the conversation about the job offer stopped there. They had wanted me to work as a technician at a lower salary than I had been earning at Edgecliff.

About ten years later, I returned to the Edgecliff campus in Cincinnati to see what had happened to the campus and the school. At the location where I had my office there was a new high rise condominium with a wonderful view overlooking the Ohio River. The Edgecliff Corbett Theater was gone—the art building was gone. The campus buildings that were farther from the bluffs were being used by the University of Cincinnati for their vocational programs. There was no Edgecliff College of Xavier University. Xavier sold the Edgecliff College campus to developers in 1987.[1] The cynics had it right.

My year at Edgecliff turned into a learning laboratory on how a college administration could manipulate an institution and an institution's faculty and students during a time of fiscal duress. All major announcements were made right before breaks when the students

---

[1] http://www.cincinnativiews.net/college_1.htm retrieved March 29, 2011.

and faculty would be leaving campus—when the social fabric of the college community would be dispersed. Major announcements were made the day before Thanksgiving break, Christmas break, and spring break. The entire faculty was notified individually, one at a time, that they were fired the day before commencement. And Xavier made a profit out of the transaction.

So this is the background story for my beginnings at SIUE.

In the fall 1980, I was one of only four faculty at new faculty orientation. I do not remember who the other three were, and I am not sure they were all faculty. Considering typical turnover rates for faculty, there would normally have been 25-30 new faculty in 1980. As a new faculty member, my focus was on getting my courses and creative activity up and running. My vision was limited to my department, my theater productions, and my classes. What I did not know until much later was that I was hired at a time when the faculty was being downsized. Without knowing it, I had come to SIUE at a time of institutional duress and change. This timing gave me the opportunity to compare how SIUE and Edgecliff College handled difficult fiscal challenges.

I had known nothing about SIUE before the summer when I applied for the position and interviewed, so I was learning as I went. Much of what I learned about SIUE beyond the bounds of the Department of Theater and Dance was spotty and had no context. For example, I met Earl Beard, the acting Provost (although the title then was acting Vice President for Academic Affairs). I did not know until later that he was a temporary administrative fill-in without roots in Academic Affairs, that he was a place marker until a new VPAA could be hired. Nor did I know the extent of administrative change that SIUE had just gone through. The previous VPAA was Earl Lazerson who had become President in 1979. John Rendleman had been the first President of SIUE until he died in 1976. In the three years between Rendleman's death and Lazerson's appointment, there were three Presidents. Two served less than a year each, and the third, Buzz Shaw, served only two years because he became Chancellor of the SIU system in 1979. That is when Lazerson became SIUE's President. With Lazerson came stability and a sense of reality. To understand what reality means here, we need to look back at how SIUE got to where it was in 1980.

SIUE started out with two locations, East St. Louis and Alton, with fewer than 2000 students. The number of students increased each year until 1970. Enrollment peaked twice over 13,000 students, first in 1970 and again in 1975. In the 13 years between 1957 and 1970, enrollment increased an average of 50% per year. These were heady times. But from 1975 until 1980, on-campus enrollment dropped 20%, and total enrollment dropped 23%.[2] This was at a time in Illinois when state university budgets were compared according to something called normative cost. As long as SIUE stayed within 5% of its normative cost in comparison with other state universities, then everything was as it should be and there would be no budget adjustments. If the enrollment changed while everything else stayed the same, then the normative costs inversely tracked the enrollment changes, not exactly but pretty closely. Because SIUE's enrollment dropped over 20%, normative costs increased well outside of the 5% window. Consequently, the Illinois Board of Higher Education (IBHE) reduced SIUE's budget for a series of years until SIUE got back within the 5% window. Earl Lazerson's first challenge as President was how to deal with a shrinking budget, which of course meant downsizing SIUE. No one likes downsizing.

At SIUE, downsizing during the 1980's was spread across the University affecting almost every department. Between 1979 and 1986, the full-time faculty decreased by over 20% with a

Earl Lazerson

PHOTOGRAPH COURTESY OF
PHOTOGRAPHIC SERVICES
COLLECTION, UNIVERSITY
ARCHIVES, LOVEJOY LIBRARY.

---

[2] *Fact Book—2011 Edition.* http://www.siue.edu/factbook/pdf/FbCurrent.pdf, p. 34. Retrieved April 11, 2011.

7% decrease in 1982 alone. When I was to become Dean of the School of Fine Arts and Communications in 1991, I met with each department chair individually and asked each one about the main challenges that their department faced. Every one of the chairs said the major challenge was that the department had been downsized, the size of the faculty was smaller than it had once been, and they were having difficulty staffing all of the courses they had created. The solution from each chair's perspective was additional faculty. I suspect every department that had been downsized, which would have been most if not all departments at SIUE, would have felt the same way. Downsizing hurts. We tend to think that size and quality connect, so if a faculty position is not refilled then the quality of the program is threatened. However, after my experiences at three very small, very high quality programs—Edgecliff College mentioned above plus Oberlin College where I was a student before transferring to Berkeley in 1968 and Whitman College where I served as technical director for a year before graduate school—I could not accept the argument that size and quality are necessarily connected. I did not tell the department chairs that, of course, and it was clear that the departments were all very strong even with the reduced size. But downsizing is always loaded with meaning. If a dean (or provost) decides not to refill a position, then that decision is interpreted as a lack of valuing, that the dean must not support or care about the program, and that negative interpretation is very real and nontrivial. Enrollment changes brought about budget changes, and the resulting downsizing affected both morale and trust.

But Earl Lazerson's challenges were not just limited to enrollment and budget. Lazerson inherited a vision of SIUE that was simply not possible in the fiscal and political climate that SIUE confronted in 1980. In the late 1960's and early 1970's, there was a vision that SIUE would become a major research university with an array of doctoral programs. Faculty members were recruited on that promise. When it became clear during the latter 1970's that SIUE was not going to become a research university, a number of faculty members felt they had been recruited with false promises, a recruiting bait and switch. They had been recruited with one set of promises, but reality turned out to be something else. Buzz Shaw had tried to sell a different vision for SIUE—the best of its kind. But for faculty who had been recruited to build doctoral programs, this new vision was not fulfilling. While not true of all faculty, a significant number of faculty members felt betrayed because the future of SIUE was not to become a research university. And Lazerson needed to confront the change in mission during budget reductions and downsizing, with a significant portion of the faculty that did not support those changes.

Because I joined the faculty at a transition point when the department had already decided to close its master's program, I knew that the Department of Theater and Dance put a focus on undergraduate education. I was not recruited to create graduate programs, and I was OK with that. While I do not know the dates or the details, one of Lazerson's early initiatives as President was to work with the faculty to create a new Mission Statement for SIUE. That new Mission Statement put first priority on undergraduate education. Because I came in at this point, I had no way of knowing that this was a change from earlier expectations and a political hot potato.

While I knew nothing of the political struggles that were going on concerning a change of mission, I did learn early on about the budget crunch. My second year (1981), I designed the lighting for the department's production of *Lysistrata*, and that design earned a national award. Because of that recognition, I got the opportunity to serve the United States Institute for Theater Technology (USITT) as a Vice Commissioner where I helped coordinate the 1983 and 1984 USITT national conference programs for lighting. Unfortunately, the department budget during fiscal year 1983 was so tight that the phones were pulled out of faculty offices, so I did not have an office phone for a few years. At that time, the only ways to communicate with the presenters for the national conference were via mail or by phone. Professional theater designers are very busy people who spend their time on the road. Mail was not an effective way to communicate because I did not know in advance what the presenters' mailing addresses might be at any given time. So without mail being viable, the telephone was the primary means of communication, but of course I did not have a phone in my office. There were several times when a call came in from New York or Seattle or Texas, or Vancouver, Canada, to one of the few department phones, and someone had to come to my office to get me so I could take the phone call. Needless to say, this was an irritant. With the ease of Internet communication and the cell phone now, we sometimes forget that it has not always been this way. Fortunately, everything ended up working out OK. But SIUE's budget challenges were not abstract for me. They were concrete, and something that I confronted almost every day.

I was quickly going to learn much more about SIUE than I could have anticipated. Two things happened in the early 1980's to get me out of my departmental and disciplinary box, and I do not remember which came first: the battle for collective bargaining or membership on the Faculty Senate.

My office was on the second floor of the Communications Building (now named Dunham Hall), hidden at the back of a small suite of offices. It had the usual desk, filing cabinet, and bookshelves, but because I was a designer, the office also had a drawing table. I spent hours and hours working on the drawing table almost every week. Students could drop in and talk while I was drawing, as could faculty. One day, Marcus Albrecht came into my office. He was a staff member from the Illinois Education Association, about which I knew nothing at the time. Marc mostly asked questions, and we talked about my experiences at Edgecliff College and what was happening at SIUE. I learned that there was a campaign for collective bargaining that had started on campus. I had no beef with SIUE, and I was anything but bitter. I was quite happy here, even though I would have liked to have had a phone, but I did have a bias in support of unions in part because unions are very important for protecting the rights of professional theater artists against unscrupulous or incompetent producers. I am a member of United Scenic Artists 829 as a lighting designer. Also, my father-in-law was a coal miner, and I had learned how much the United Mine Workers had been able to improve mine safety in the United States and to help miners earn a living wage. So when Mark and I talked, it made sense for me to support faculty collective bargaining, particularly after my experiences at Edgecliff College where faculty members had been isolated and easily manipulated.

Mark invited me to a meeting of the IEA-NEA Organizing Committee. I went to the meeting and got involved. To make a long story short, I ended up as co-chair of the organizing committee with Bill Feeney as the other co-chair by the time of the election. For the first vote, 60% of the faculty voted in favor of collective bargaining, and 40% voted against, or in other words, for No Agent. The 60% vote supporting collective bargaining was an indication of the faculty dissatisfaction with the ways things were going at SIUE. But the faculty voting in favor almost exactly split between the Illinois Education Association (IEA) and the Illinois Federation of Teachers (IFT) with close to 30% for each. The IEA received a few more votes than the IFT and faced a run off election with No Agent. Unfortunately for those who supported collective bargaining, the battle between the IEA and the IFT on campus had been contentious and sometimes just plain nasty. The IFT had been around for years before the IEA started on campus, so a number of the IFT faculty had very negative feelings about the IEA—the interlopers. The end result is that not enough of the IFT supporters voted for the IEA. Even though 60% of the faculty supported collective bargaining in the first vote, less than 50% supported the IEA in the run off.

The result of the election in favor of No Agent was not only a consequence of rivalry between the IEA and the IFT. Other things were happening at SIUE, too. First, the budget pressures of downsizing in the early 1980's had started to reverse. Second, Earl Lazerson established a million dollar fund for Excellence in Undergraduate Education in 1986 by reallocating from administrative functions. Third, there was a change of the chief academic officer in 1987 when David

SIUE Faculty Organizing Committee, IEA-NEA:
Committee co-chairs Professor William Feeney (Political Science), left,
and Assoc. Prof. David Sill (Theater and Dance), center.
Also pictured: Assoc. Professor Richard McKinney (Management).
PHOTOGRAPH BY DAVID VITOFF COURTESY OF THE ILLINOIS EDUCATION ASSOCIATION ARCHIVES.

Werner became Provost. Barbara Teeters, the previous Vice President for Academic Affairs, presided over some very difficult budgetary decisions. She had neither ties to nor support from the faculty in part because she had been an external candidate for the position and in part because she did nothing to develop ties with the faculty. Plus she got the blame for the downsizing decisions even though many of those decisions were made by the Deans or the President, not the VPAA. Werner, in contrast, came from the faculty and had served successfully as Dean of the School of Business. He had faculty roots at SIUE and was both well liked and well respected by the faculty. Furthermore, faculty played a meaningful role in the selection process for Werner including rewriting the position description and the title. And Werner was not forced to downsize academic programs as Provost. The Faculty Senate had grown strong and was taking leadership on issues important to the faculty. These changes happened before the final collective bargaining election in 1988.

After the election, Lazerson individually met with Bill Feeney and with me to talk about both the past and the future. He listened to our concerns and the reasons that we had supported collective bargaining. Fortunately, in my case, the reasons that I supported collective bargaining were historical and pragmatic. There was nothing either emotional or personal behind why I joined the IEA effort and why I served as co-chair of the organizing committee. It made the talk with Lazerson easy, relaxed, and non-threatening. Feeney had a similar experience. There were several of our concerns that Lazerson addressed, and neither Bill Feeney nor I ever had any repercussions for having led the IEA organizing effort. Many in the faculty were surprised and some were shocked when I was appointed Acting Dean of the School of Fine Arts and Communications three years after co-chairing the IEA Organizing Committee. SIUE as a community, as an organization, as a culture, had the capacity to keep the focus on what was important and move forward without staying tied up in the past.

Both before and after the collective bargaining vote, Lazerson met periodically in his office on Friday afternoons with a group of faculty leaders, such as former Faculty Senate Presidents and chairs of the University Planning and Budget Council (UPBC), to discuss the big issues concerning SIUE and higher education, visioning for the future. These are the same issues that Lazerson discussed with Bill Feeney and me—What is the future? What are the trends? What should we be doing? How could we do it better? Lazerson not only listened to faculty but also engaged and empowered them, putting faculty into meaningful decision-making positions. During the critical years between 1985 and 1990, the Faculty Senate participated in planning and approving all major decisions, including those regarding curriculum, programs, dean selection, assessment, and faculty equity raises. While Lazerson's administration opposed a faculty union, ultimately the administration and the institution responded constructively in the aftermath of the campaign for collective bargaining. The result was that SIUE grew stronger and was able to respond to the political pressures from outside the University in ways that most other institutions were not able to do.

For example, in the middle 1980's there were multiple calls for some kind of assessment of student learning in higher education. The SIUE Faculty Senate made a commitment to developing an assessment plan as early as 1985. By 1989, the University Assessment Plan was approved and implemented, with David Steinberg serving as the first Director of Undergraduate Assessment beginning in January 1990. In the year that SIUE's Assessment Plan was approved, 1989, the Illinois Board of Higher Education (IBHE) called for public universities to consider beginning the development of assessment programs, and also in 1989 the Higher Learning Commission of the North Central Association of Schools and Colleges (HLC, NCA) for the first time announced that assessment would be expected for accreditation. In other words, SIUE's Faculty Senate and administration had already completed development and was implementing an assessment program in 1989 at the time when IBHE and HLC announced that institutions should start thinking about assessment. That put SIUE ahead of the curve where it has stayed. Other institutions have struggled to implement meaningful assessment programs, and it is not unusual for institutions in 2011, over twenty years later, to run into trouble with reaffirmation of accreditation because they have yet to fully implement an assessment program.[3] Over those twenty years, SIUE has been in a position of leadership in assessment with IBHE, HLC, and the higher education professional organizations such as the American Association of Higher Education (AAHE),

---

[3] For the past ten years I have served the Higher Learning Commission as an Academic Quality Improvement Program (AQIP) peer reviewer including serving on the Admissions Panel. The institutions that apply for admission to AQIP tend to be more likely to have developed assessment programs than those institutions that do not apply. Yet the majority of applications indicated that the institutions were having challenges implementing assessment programs even though they had been required to have assessment programs for over fifteen years.

the American Association of Colleges and Universities (AAC&U), and the American Association of State Colleges and Universities (AASCU). SIUE was able to take what could have been negative, as developing assessment has been experienced by most institutions, and find ways to use assessment to support our mission and purpose, to make it meaningful for us.

In spite of, or perhaps because of, the struggles at SIUE during the 1980's with budget cuts, collective bargaining, and refocusing the mission on undergraduate education, the SIUE community was positioned to achieve and succeed at challenges in Higher Education that other institutions could not solve. By 1990, SIUE had an established assessment program and a marque Excellence in Undergraduate Education grant program. The assessment program energized curricular and programmatic improvements, and the EUE grants encouraged individual faculty development and creativity. In addition, SIUE has had a combination of programs, policies, and practices that helped develop a strong sense of common community on campus allowing SIUE to work toward institutional goals rather than fracturing into disciplinary silos, which are common for medium sized universities. For example, SIUE has had a long term Interdisciplinary Studies (IDS) general education requirement that is team taught, pairing faculty with other faculty from outside their own departments. The effect of this pairing of faculty is subtle and powerful involving 5-10% of the faculty each year. Assessment, EUE, IDS, and meaningful faculty input into decision making through the Faculty Senate and UPBC have helped build community.

Returning to the beginning of this story, there was a difference between how Edgecliff College handled its economic and existential crisis and the way that SIUE handled similar challenges. At Edgecliff College, all of the decisions were made on the basis of business considerations. The Sisters of Mercy gave lip service to mission and purpose but made decisions based on ridding themselves of a financial burden. Xavier University wanted to make a profit on the transaction. The mission, the education of the students, the sustaining of the facilities and faculty that had been developed, the educational purpose for existing in the first place—all of that was forgotten when the decisions were made. In contrast, SIUE's central purpose shaped the decisions that were made in spite of the challenges. The education of students, the role of SIUE in regional service, the development of faculty, and maintenance of the facilities were never forgotten. Edgecliff College died. SIUE thrived. While one could argue that SIUE was never at risk of closing down, there is no denying that it was at risk of becoming dysfunctional and becoming less than it could be. SIUE was able to grow not just in terms of numbers but also in terms of its ability to meet its purpose during periods of challenge.

In looking at the photo of the Edgecliff Corbett Theater, my office was the window in the upper right corner. That building, the wonderful theater, and the College are no more. I wonder what might have happened if the Sisters of Mercy had remembered their reason for creating Edgecliff College in the first place and made the difficult decisions necessary to keep their original vision alive. That is in many ways what Earl Lazerson did for SIUE. And I wonder if the faculty of Edgecliff College had stood together for the values and purpose that made their work consequential, perhaps they could have helped the Sisters of Mercy with making the necessary decisions to keep the College healthy. In many ways that is what the SIUE faculty did in their struggle with collective bargaining and their leadership in the Faculty Senate.

Much of what has made SIUE the extraordinary place it is now had its roots in the difficult years from 1975-1985. Under the administrative leadership first of Buzz Shaw and then of Earl Lazerson, SIUE developed an institutional personality that approached challenges as opportunities. At the same time, SIUE would never have developed that personality without the faculty leadership that came forward during the struggle over collective bargaining and that stepped forward to serve in the Faculty Senate. In the years after David Werner was appointed Provost, SIUE pioneered initiatives that put it ahead of the curve on some of the most pressing challenges of higher education in this country. The institutional strengths that we found in 1990 grew out of the work, the vision, and dedication of a community of faculty, administrators, staff, and students working toward common purpose. This, then, was the fertile ground from which the College of Arts and Sciences grew.

Becoming an *Artist* Educator:

The Journey at SIUE

by JOSEPH A. WEBER

An artist's journey begins with the making of marks, as an infant, and drawing lines that become shapes as a toddler; these spark intrinsic connections between art expression and the world of the future artist. As a child grows and becomes more secure in communicating thoughts and feelings through symbols, the discovery of the world begins and takes on a very individual set of schemas. Later, as an elementary school student, the discovery of creating art through a variety of media and techniques is found to be personally rewarding and fulfilling. Unlike some subjects in the school curriculum, the child soon realizes that art is all about individual expression and personal problem solving. There is no right or wrong solution to an art assignment, just the student's way of expressing thoughts or ideas found within their own creativity. The student's individual ideas matter more than their classmates. Young artists find that they need to take risks to achieve the desired outcome with media. Experimenting, elaborating

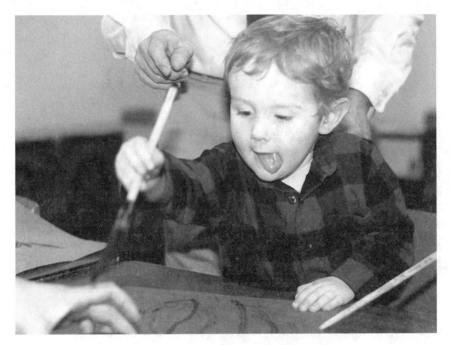

Joy of making lines by a young artist as part of an International Night at the SIUE Religious Center 1989.

PHOTOGRAPH BY JOSEPH WEBER.

and being flexible with their techniques, students discover that making art is their nonverbal way of communicating the meaning or sense of their world to themselves and others. Learning is achieved through the trial and error process, and sometimes the process is frustrating and difficult. They may need to start over with different approaches, often leading to success only the second or third time around.

Some artists first realize during their middle school or high school years, or much later as adults, that they are good at art, talented, perhaps even driven by art. They are rewarded by the gratification they get from spending time with their art. They love to make art. They discover they like to draw, paint, design, construct or model with media of all kinds. They spend time looking and studying the work of other artists and designers. They love to learn new techniques with different media. They want to draw from nature. Often they value realism. They are recognized by their teachers, parents and fellow students for their special talent. Their art work stands out above others in the class. The thought of a career in the visual arts crosses their mind more and more: do they have enough dedication and commitment to pursue this dream? Where do they go for further study? Can they imagine their life without creating art?

It is a scary time when one is contemplating a career as an artist. Many negative comments are voiced by others about such a career decision. Critics warn that it is hard to make a living as an artist, that it is not a practical career for this day and age. Artists themselves, however, report that when individual commitment and application of hard work to the study of art is made, most individuals find success either in the field or a related field of art work, and add that the study of art prepared them for many life skills, enriching their lives tremendously.

I know about such things. I lived through them as a youth. Luckily for me, I had a teacher in middle school who saw I had a real interest and potential for art. She encouraged me to pursue my talent. Although I grew up in a small town with limited resources for studying art, my teacher opened up a new world for me, a world of creating and communicating ideas through art. She showed me a way of putting meaning into my life by way of my genuine interest and thirst for art. She started me on a path of looking at and studying art as a real subject, not just as a hobby. She shared her books and supplies with me, resources I had never seen before. She stressed looking at and studying the world around me and sketching what I saw. She encouraged much practice in drawing. She introduced me to the world of two- and three- dimensional art, and the artists who had created such works. To this day, I am extremely grateful to this teacher for her dedication to her field and sharing it with others, especially a kid like me who loved art, but did not know where to go to experience and learn more. Her support and encouragement fueled my passion and whetted my appetite for art. In turn, I was hooked for life and knew some day I would do something with art.

Upon graduation from high school, I knew I was going to be an artist. I knew I could not be myself without making art. Where was I to go to further this study? I had limited resources. I knew I did not have the background preparation of some other students, but I was determined to work and learn and apply myself. I could do it! Reluctantly, my parents supported my decision.

In my research for locating a school to study art, I discovered there are basically two types of institutions. The oldest and the most traditional center for art schooling is the Fine Arts Academy or Art Institute. For centuries, artists have been trained to become fine artists in these schools. The curriculum centers on painting, drawing, sculpture and printmaking, and the courses are intense. These institutions are generally private and require acceptance by way of a portfolio. In recent years, the curriculum has been expanded to include the areas of photography, graphic design, crafts and interior design. It is an excellent setting for a very serious art student.

The second place to study art is at a college or university. Here the emphasis is not only to become trained in one or two major fields of the visual arts, but also to be exposed to the liberal arts as part of their art training. The liberal arts provide the artist with opportunities to explore themes and concepts as they relate to other art forms and the humanities. Exposure to philosophy, history, music, sociology, literature, languages and the sciences round out the artist's education, thus broadening the perspective and concepts the artist may wish to draw upon for inspiration.

At a university, future artists can assist their personal development by looking and experiencing all matter of things and subjects. They will examine their lives in the greater context of the world around them. They may learn to look and see and find meaning in the world. Ben Shahn, a prominent American artist in the 20th century, whose work is included in museums around the world, was asked to deliver a series of lectures at Harvard University on art education. His views were published in his book, *The Shape of Content* in the late 1950's. His recommendation for the individual interested in art pursue an education is as follows:

Attend a university if you possibly can. There is no content of knowledge that is not pertinent to the work you will want to do. But before you attend a university work at something for a while. Do anything. Get a job in a potato field; or work as a grease-monkey in an auto repair shop. But if you do work in a field do not fail to observe the look and the feel of earth and of all things that you handle—yes, even potatoes! Or, in the auto shop, the smell of oil and grease and burning rubber. Paint of course, but if you have to lay aside paintings for a time, continue to draw. Listen well to all conversations and be instructed by them and take all seriousness seriously. Never look down upon anything or anyone as not worthy of notice. In college or out of college, read. And form opinions! Read Sophocles and Euripedes and Dante and Proust. Read everything that you can find about art except the reviews. Read the Bible; read Hume; read Pogo. Read all kinds of poetry and know many poems and many artists. Go to an art school, or two, or three, or take art courses at night if necessary. And paint and paint and draw and draw. Know all that you can, both curricular and noncurricular—mathematics and physics and economics, logic, and particularly history. Know at least two languages besides your own, but anyway, know French. Look at pictures and more pictures. Look at every kind of visual symbol, every kind of emblem; do not spurn signboards or furniture drawings or this style of art or that style of art. Do not be afraid to like paintings honestly or to dislike them honestly, but if you do dislike them retain an open mind. Do not dismiss any school of art, not the Pre-Raphaelites nor the Hudson River School nor the German Genre painters. Talk and talk and sit at cafes, and listen to everything, to Brahms, to Brubeck, to the Italian hour on the radio. Listen to preachers in small town churches and in big city churches. Listen to politicians in New England town meetings and to rabble-rousers in Alabama. Even draw them. And remember that you are trying to learn to think what you want to think, that you are trying to coordinate mind and hand and eye. Go to all sorts of museums and galleries and to the studios of artists. Go to Paris and Madrid and Rome and Ravenna and Padua. Stand alone in Sainte Chapelle, in the Sistine Chapel, in the Church of the Carmine in Florence. Draw and draw and paint and learn to work in many media; try lithography and aquatint and silk-screen. Know all that you can about art, and by all means have opinions. Never be afraid to become embroiled in art or life or politics; never be afraid to learn to draw or paint better than you already do; and never be afraid to undertake any kind of art at all, however exalted or however common, but do it with distinction. (Shahn 130-131)

Ben Shahn emphasized to those future students of art the need to develop a perspective on life and engage in the act of sensing the world through many different experiences. These experiences, along with formal art training becomes the unique expression and content of the artist. In order to fully experience life, an artist must embrace the objective and subjective aspects of the experience. The artist eventually becomes comfortable with processing the essence of the experiences that becomes one's art. The feelings, ideas and beliefs that are communicated through media and subject matter evolve into art. This is a lifelong process. As long as you consider yourself an artist, inspiration that comes from your personal encounters with the world, becomes the themes of your work. I believe Ben Shahn's words are as important today as they were in the 1950's, and the university can provide many of these needed experiences and the food for thought. It has taken me forty years of teaching to understand that artists must be constantly open to the experiences of daily life and that these experiences are the sum and substance of their unique interpretation of their world that becomes their art. This is what makes art, art; however, at the root of it all, the individual artist must be open to new encounters with ideas, places and things and be open to see, not just to look. It was my role as artist and teacher to be the catalyst for this to occur.

Over the course of my professional career, I have attended a variety of art schools, both private and public, academies and universities, and experienced many different philosophic and aesthetic approaches. As a result, I have developed a view of art education for the future artist to consider. I believe one must find the best fit for their art education based on their personal characteristics. The confident, secure, focused student will find an academy the perfect place for their education. They will thrive on the rigor and competition. The individual who loves art, but who is also nurtured by information and knowledge in other fields of the humanities, and who may not have a specific focus in the visual arts as yet, will find the options at the university appealing to their development. Like Ben Shahn, I believe the university setting and its curriculum broadens the artist to think in different ways and create art based on the inspiration found in many areas of life. Here there are opportunities for exploration before settling on a major art area. In either case, artists must be very dedicated and immerse themselves into their studies completely. In each educational setting, one will need to spend enormous amounts of time working in and out of the studio to achieve the results required by the different art disciplines.

The study of art is the pursuit of skills and techniques with media that culminate in the communication of ideas. All professions in visual art share this goal. For art students this is the overall quest. Yet the field of art is broad and has application to many forms and people. The degree programs in the Department of Art and Design at SIUE, provide for such approaches. Some art students want more from their studies in art. They want to use art and the art process to help others grow and develop as human beings. They see art as a major contributor to the general education of all people. Art helps with the development of problem solving skills, visual perception skills, and divergent thinking strategies. Becoming an art educator is how they see their future using their love of art. Others may see the value of the art and the art making process helpful with individuals that need psychological support. Individuals suffering from emotional and physical injuries can use Art Therapy to assist in their illness and wellness approaches, making this field a very intriguing and demanding choice for the advanced art student to consider. Some art students like the history of art and how art has been used and is currently being used to inform us of the people and times in which it was created. Humanity has created art for centuries and art historians shed light on specific times in history, exploring peoples' cultures and values. Some art students choose to study art history, in addition to some courses in studio art, to more fully comprehend the past as it relates to the present. Perhaps the art museum is a place where they would like to work one day.

SIUE offers students the opportunities to study art in the Department of Art and Design where they can concentrate in any of these fields of concentration. The Art and Design faculty all have terminal degrees in their specialized teaching fields. They set the standards high for themselves and their students. They demand the highest from themselves and their students. When students apply themselves, they usually achieve success. The degree programs attempt to present many connections between the fine arts and the liberal arts as part of their education as an artist. It is important to remember that at the basis of all art education is the acquisition of the knowledge of art and skills in art making, to understand how life affects ones art and to be proficient in communicating these thoughts through ones art.

Working at SIUE over many years has reinforced my position that one of the reasons for the success of its programs and students in Art and Design is its location. SIUE is located near a major metropolitan area and cultural center: St. Louis, Missouri. The metro area provides access to art exhibits, museums, other university art programs and cultural venues for enrichment in the field of art studies. It provides exhibition space and a wider audience base for the art student to exhibit his work besides the university setting. For education and art therapy students, there are a wide range of clinical schools and centers for practicums. That professional support, by the educators and clinicians in these centers, allows for a true firsthand perspective by our students to see and participate in working programs prior to graduation. As a result, upon graduation from SIUE, students are prepared to begin work in the real world. Within thirty minutes of campus students can experience art in galleries and museums, participate in urban, suburban and rural school districts as well as have access to major medical and mental health centers. In my opinion, this is the best of all possible worlds; a wonderful quality and diverse art program in a university setting, along with access to a broad and rich major cultural resource center.

Another plus for SIUE is the campus environment. The campus environment, to anyone who is interested in places that inspire thinking and study, where art and architecture are combined with nature, is an excellent example of design and nature working together to create a harmonious whole. This was by design. The academic buildings and roadways into the campus are surrounded by nature. Nature changes from season to season bringing colors and shapes into the daily lives of its students and faculty. Original art is placed everywhere on campus. Art can be found in student centers, classrooms, libraries, residence halls and all over the outdoor plazas and walkways. The art is by noted artists and SIUE students. The buildings in the main academic core reflect the Prairie Style of architecture named after Frank Lloyd Wright. These long, large, asymmetrical buildings, constructed of natural material, hug the landscape as to become one with the land. In each building there are places for quiet study and reflection, outside and inside, where thinking and reading is available. The architectural firm of Hellmuth, Obata and Kassabaum designed the main campus core. They worked with the landscape firm of Sasaki, Dawson and DeMay Associates on the design of the twenty-six hundred acre campus site. The campus has grown and matured since the 1960s, but the campus is, in my opinion, one of the most beautiful in the USA. I never got tired of going to campus because the beauty of the place always inspired me.

The typical art student I taught while at SIUE came from the metro area. When I left the university, more students were enrolled from all parts of Illinois and Missouri because of the new residence halls. Graduate students too were coming from other states and parts of the world to study art at SIUE. The department offered undergraduate degrees in many fields of study: BFA and BA in Art Studio, BS in Art Education, BA in Art History. On the graduate level there was a MFA in Art Studio, MA in Art Therapy and the MS in Secondary Education, Art Education. I was very pleased to have played a major role in the Art Education program. My philosophy as I approached the curriculum for the future artist-educator was to put a heavy emphasis on studio art development along with a general sound foundation in art history. Teaching method courses stressed an understanding of aesthetics, developmental psychology, curriculum design and clinical practicums in real classrooms with real students. In addition, students' academic performance would be evaluated and then assessed. They would also need to participate in 100 hours of clinical observations and experience prior to student teaching. The result was a student, competent in the studio arts, who had an understanding of cultures and history and an understanding of the developmental needs of the students they would teach. Students performed well and as a result were hired in many school districts all over the metro area and Midwest. Some went on to teach in Australia, Guam and Russia as well as on several Native American reservations in the US. More and more graduate students went on to get their doctorates in Art Education and are teaching in major universities in the US. I could not be prouder of their accomplishments and the art education programs at SIUE.

I am especially proud to have had a hand in developing the MA in Art Therapy at SIUE. Because of its regional location and mission, SIUE was a perfect fit for the Art Therapy program. This graduate program now has produced therapists, who are working all over the world, that use art as another vehicle for human development and well being. SIUE's Art Therapy program is a leader in the field. The Art Department too has extended its resources to area schools by exhibiting student's art work and conducting workshops and demonstrations on campus for elementary and secondary students. Leading Art Educators have given lectures and demonstration on campus to our students and area educators. Many partnerships have been created between local schools, clinics and museums for our students to gain valuable "hands on" experiences.

Having confidence in the caliber of students graduating from these programs, I began to look at other opportunities SIUE could offer to further enhance our students' experience. One thing I have noticed was a lack of travel to other countries by our SIUE students.

They had little to no firsthand exposure to other cultures, especially to European countries. I felt this was unfortunate because Europe housed so much art our students encountered in their art history studies. Art educators build into their curricula all types of art historical information, yet most of our students have never seen the originals they use as examples in their classroom. Furthermore, to see the art and architecture of a given country where it was created and to experience the culture of the people who created it was essential to the meaning of the art work itself. Therefore I proposed, during my last year at SIUE, an early summer trip to England, France and the Netherlands for our students. Thirty-six students registered for the trip. The trip was customized so students had tours of various art museums and art centers with locally trained art historians. The students also had free time to explore cities on their own. We stayed in out-of-the-way hotels so the students had to learn to ride the public transportation and encounter different languages. They visited London, the National Gallery, the Tate and Tate Modern and other points of interest including the night life of London. We took a fast train to Paris and spent time at the Louvre, Musse d'Orsay and Pompidou Centre as well a wonderful side trip to Monet's Giverny. Time was also spent in Paris exploring the city and its

The painting, The Three Graces by Baron Jean Baptiste Gegnault 1754-1829, in the Louvre Museum, Paris, is graced by the three graces from SIUE, Lynn North, Kim Lemmon-Lebar and Roberta Springer, graduate students and teachers, 2004.

PHOTOGRAPH BY LYNN NORTH.

restaurants. In Amsterdam the students visited the Rijksuseum, the Van Gogh Museum and a special visit to a university art school where artists like themselves were studying to be art teachers. The school was called the Academie voor Beeldende Vorming. This is one of two academies in the Netherlands that train teachers in art. We spent the morning talking with the faculty and students at the Academie. We found that we had a lot in common. Their studio arts, like those of SIUE, are of high quality and students need to be proficient in one or two areas. For art educators, as in the US, culture and art historical information was a major part of all lessons in the Netherlands. This was the highlight of the trip to hear and see and share ideas and thoughts about teaching art from and in a European country.

As part of the requirement for the trip, students needed to create a series of art work based on their experiences in these three countries, using whatever media they wanted. In addition the students needed to research an artist about whom they previously had no knowledge. The art work, both two and three dimensional with multimedia approaches, was exhibited in the Wagner Gallery in the Art and Design building. We hosted a reception for the students, their parents and friends and the university community. The event was a huge success and a wonderful capstone to the experience. Several of our graduates, now art teachers on the secondary level, have taken their own students to Europe, after their SIUE trip, thus planting the seed for further cultural exploration.

As my teaching career came to an end at SIUE, I felt terribly proud and personally rewarded by the years spent working in the Art and Design Department with the students and faculty. SIUE gave me the freedom and opportunity to grow professionally and create the types of programs I felt were needed for the demands of our time and for the professional development of our students. We were able to develop partnerships with many schools in the area. Our students had opportunities to teach art in real classrooms while studying art on campus. We were far ahead of the times with this model of training artist-teachers, now required by the State for all certification programs. Years later, many of our former students, now teachers, are making major contributions to their students, their schools and their communities. It is very gratifying to hear from them. They express their gratitude for the efforts made on their behalf while students at SIUE. They say how rewarded they are with the decision they made in becoming an artist-educator and in studying art at SIUE. Their journey came to a successful conclusion!

The challenges of teaching at the university level are many, but with the challenges come opportunities. I found myself to be a better professor, artist, citizen and humanitarian because of working at SIUE with my students and colleagues. To me SIUE was and is always a special place. The journey was very rewarding!

For Further Reading

Bersson, Robert. *Responding to Art: Form, Content, and Context.* New York: McGraw Hill, 2004.

Dewey, John. *Art As Experience.* New York: Perigee Book, 1934.

Eisner, Elliot W. *The Kind of Schools We Need: Personal Essays.* Portsmouth, New Hampshire: Heinemann, 1998.

Gardner, Howard. *The Arts and Human Development.* New York: Perseus books Group, 1994.

Gardner, Howard. *Art, Mind and Brain: A Cognitive Approach to Creativity.* New York, New York: Basic Books, Inc., Publishers, 1982.

Henri, Robert. *The Art Spirit.* Philadelphia, Pennsylvania: J. B. Lippincott Company, 1923.

Rhyne, Jane. *The Gestalt Art Experience: Creative Process and Expressive Therapy.* Chicago, Illinois: Magnolia Street Publishers, 1984.

Shahn, Ben. *The Shape of Content.* New York: Vintage Books, 1957.

Smith, Ralph. *Aesthetics and Criticism in Art Education.* Chicago, Illinois: Rand McNally and Company, 1966.

Walling, Donovan R. *Under Construction: The Role of the Arts and Humanities in Postmodern Schools.* Bloomington, Indiana: Phi Delta Kappa Educational Foundation, 1997.

S-I-U-E... & ME...

by EUGENE B. REDMOND

SIUE alumnus, emeritus professor of English and, since 1976, poet laureate of East St. Louis (Il)

Eugene B. Redmond serving as a student leader during freshman orientation at SIU-E, 1961.

PHOTOGRAPH COURTESY OF PHOTOGRAPHIC SERVICES COLLECTION, UNIVERSITY ARCHIVES, LOVEJOY LIBRARY.

(This prose poem was delivered as the SIUE commencement address in May of 2008 when Eugene B. Redmond received an Honorary Doctor of Humane Letters Degree.)

My courtship with SIUE began in 1957 when I finished Lincoln Senior High School and the Metro-East Campus of SIU—initially without the "E"—was born in the threefold womb of Alton–East St. Louis–Edwardsville. We were an "extension" of Carbondale.

Permit me to conjure that year in a poetic form called the "Kwansaba"…

> As a quiet coup, S-I-U yawned in
> > noisy 1957—a sandwich-year between Korea
> & Vietnam, spiced with Space Age Sputnik
> > & Elliott Rudwick, Elvis & Miles, Little
> Rock 9 & hoola hoop grind, led
> > by Emmett Till & Rosa Parks' Montgomery
> sparks, amidst bid whist & the Twist.

In 1958, an infant SIU (E) & I separated when the Marine Corps offered me free travel to exotic places like San Diego (for boot camp), Hawaii, Okinawa, Japan, Hong Kong, Southeast Asia, & Quantico, Virginia. After my discharge in early 1961, we (still known as "Salukis") danced again at the East St. Louis Center a. k. a. "Tenth Street Tech." Extracurricularly, I acted in plays with the Neo-Thalesians, wrote for three local weeklies newspapers (& one daily), became editor of the *Alestle,* & attended the 1963 March on Washington where Martin Luther King Jr. gave his "I Have a Dream" speech.

1963 "memwar": an imperfect Kwansaba...

> We were mere hyper-active students, debatin'
> Nuclear War & Civil Rights, Greek Drama
> & Women's Lib, MLK's Big March &
> JFK's New Frontier, The Other America &
> Catch 22—until bullets, raining on Kennedy
> in Dallas, drained East Saint Louis of
> its Light—but what did we know?

Energized by resident literati, campus visits by renowned poets like W. H. Auden & John Logan, & editorial work with *The Three Penny Broadside & Sou'wester* magazines, I was baptized in the four genres of writing—drama, fiction, nonfiction, & poetry. Poetry, the most concentrated, expresses life in rhythm & music. It also operates in mysterious—even mystical & magical—ways.

While some of you may find it impossible to envision a world & time before

> S-I-U-E Began Its 50-Year Feast
> Among the Gardens of Metro East,
> the following pastiche of the four genres,
> anchored in poetry, aims to do just that...
>
> O Background! O Foreground! O Ritualground!
>
> Before University came Communiversity
> spirit village before human spillage
> naturefication before urbanization
> beauty's elevation before ugly's escalation
> soul-arts before flesh darts
> variegation before segregation

Over wars race-riots floods strikes quakes-of-earth & tornado alleys Forebears fashioned ancestrails...

& lo, an indo-ethno-socio gumbo...

Cahokia Mounds & sacred grounds...immigrants & indigents...
 [middle passage express & underground conch/us/nests]...ethnic creeds
& abductees...gothic gables & streetcar cables...garlic breaths & TB deaths
 onion fingers & doo wop singers...blues guitars & used slop jars
fiddles & skittles...see-saw & pre-law...low gas lamps & red-light vamps
 scripture reader & animal breeder...lollypop/s & hot bebop/s
dough kneader & Deutsh lieder...baklava & hot java...beer songs
 & ice tongs...brassy jazzers & razmatazzers...gospel & polka...hostel
& mocha...

Let's taste one cultural ingredient of this gumbo...

"East Saint Arkansippi Winter Fest"

Amidst ample helpings of snow,
 We break wood & lumps of coal, repair socks & souls,
Light candles & kerosene lamps,
 Brim with homework & biblical verses,
Inhale kitchen sauces "collard" by greens until...
 African nightfires dance & cackle/dance & cackle,
& our neon bodies are Kwanzaa/Xmas Trees
 Brushing against walls of the dark...
Now, children of the *whirl,*
 Come! Congregate, shed sweat with us,
& *swirl swirl swirl swirl...*

SIUE & I parted a second time in 1964 when I graduated & entered grad school at Washington U in the Lou; but, we resumed our courtship in 1967, the year I returned to Tenth Street Tech & became a Teacher-Counselor in the Experiment in Higher Education (EHE), a revolutionary & successful program for high school graduates not deemed college worthy. That same year, Katherine Dunham set up her Performing Arts Training Center (PATC) where I also taught & served as a Senior Consultant. But alas, two years later, we split a third time when I became Writer-in-Residence at Oberlin College in Ohio &, a year later, joined my favorite teacher, Vernon "Ted" Hornback, on the faculty at California State University Sacramento.

Kwansaba for Mentor "Ted":
    He was Beowulf & Bohemia, Roland &
    Siegfried, King Arthur & King Oliver, Chaucer &
    Satchmo, fluent in Latin & Nipponese, lit
    up like Gas Light Square & Faulkner's
    Bear—Ted, who held fast to steins,
    stems of wine, e.e. cummings, Langston's
    hues &, like homeboy Miles, all blues.

Eugene B. Redmond with SIU-E English teacher/mentor Vernon T. (Ted) Hornback (1931–2005) in 1968 at California State University Sacramento (where EBR joined VTH on faculty in 1970).
PHOTOGRAPH BY DUANE SPILLSBURY CSUS NEWS SERVICES.

Returning home to East St. Louis in the mid-1980's, I resumed my romance with SIU-"E" in 1990—& am now embarking upon a fourth separation as a retiree.

Following is an Ancestral "Collection," Selected/Beloved teachers, classmates, friends, & colleagues whose paths intersected mine at SIU-"E"...

Joyce Aschenbrenner, a "familistic" scholar & teacher, arrived from Chicago—in the late 1960's—to teach in EHE & PATC. During the 70's, 80's, 90's & 2000's, she recorded urban anthropology & Dunham's legacy in numerous articles & books.

Affectionately known as "B-witz," *William C. Benowitz* was a true esthete, a colorful, effective-effete teacher who brilliantly mixed Shakespeare & current news in textbooks he wrote for his math classes. We feared & revered "B-witz."

You couldn't be mentally lazy around classmate/friend *Raymond Campbell,* photographer, tennis coach, & dance-floor wizard. In 1962, Ray, his mother, his sister Selena, his ring-bearer-nephew Wesley, & I drove to Dallas, Texas, where I was best man in Ray's wedding. Because Southern restaurants, hotels, & motels did not serve Black people, the women prepared fried chicken & wrapped it in cellophane for the trip. Ray & I slept on the ground at night, keeping one open eye on the women & boy in the car.

Rearranging his nickname, "Hank," to form the anagram, "Ankh," name of the Egyptian symbol for the cross & eternal life, writer *Henry Dumas,* my "inventive" colleague in EHE, also spelled his last name backwards to create "Samud." Called "an absolute genius" by Nobel Laureate Toni Morrison, Dumas summed up the creation in a couplet titled "Funk":

> The great god Shango in the African sea
> reached down with palm oil and oozed out me.

2008 marks the 40th anniversary of Dumas' death & of my executorship of his literary estate. His posthumously published books include *Ark of Bones and Other Stories* (SIUC Press), *Jonoah and the Green Stone* (a novel from Random House), *Knees of a Natural Man* (poems from Thunder's Mouth Press) & *Echo Tree* (stories from Coffee House Press).

And now, a Kwansaba for Katherine Dunham's rendezvous with SIU:

>With Marlene Dietrich & French dancer Mistinguette,
>she had "one of the three best
>sets of legs in the world," this
>Duke Ellington of Dance! What her moves
>meant in Port Au Prince, Paris, Dakar
>& East St. Louis—lives in lithe
>dreams, walking drums, child-eyes, Dunham Hall.

Eugene B. Redmond with Katherine Dunham (1909–2006) in 1985 at the KD Museum in East St. Louis.
PHOTOGRAPH BY SHERMAN L. FOWLER.

Another Visionary, *R. Buckminster Fuller*—or "Bucky"—was a poet, scientist, inventor, architect, futurist, & designer of the geodesic dome. Examples of his genius are SIUE's Religious Center & the Mary Brown Center in East St. Louis' Lincoln Park.

Good friend *Joseph E. Harrison,* also a 1960's student leader, became an EHE Teacher-Counselor, a precinct committeeman, licensed pilot, & board member of East St. Louis' Olatunji Tutoring & Placement Center.

Also a Renaissance man, *Emil Jason,* directed the East St. Louis Center, Chaired SIUE's Chemistry Department, and was an inventor and organizer of farmers recalling M.B.Tolson, the great poet & professor portrayed by Denzel Washington in the movie, "The Great Debaters."

Taylor Jones III was another brilliant student leader &, later, a navigator for the Congress of Racial Equality (CORE). Katherine Dunham memorialized him in "The Ode to Taylor Jones III," a multimedia ballet that toured the Midwest & East Coast including 16 high schools in Connecticut.

Leonard Long, chemist & coalition builder like Dunham, Fuller & Jones, helped anchor the student body at Tenth Street Tech. He later worked for Monsanto Chemical Company & conducted studies on lead poisoning in Metro East communities before teaching in EHE and the Environmental Sciences Programs.

Noah Lucatz, who held the Adam Smith Chair of Political Economy at the University of Glasgow in Scotland, was a visiting professor at the East St. Louis Center. Under him, I studied the "Politics of Underdevelopment" & the Third World. But I also had the job, opportunity really, of "collecting" him—as he put it—from his downtown St. Louis apartment. During those daily drives to &

from the campus, our conversations were worth their time & gas in intellectual gold.

Ina Peabody Sledge's rendezvous with SIU began as a student in the 1960's & ended as a faculty member in Lovejoy Library. In a poem, I eulogized this sophisticated lady as a "modest jazzologist" who

> carried Bird, Billie & Miles on her tongue
> & volumes of Ellington in her hum
>
> ...balancing libraries & blues,
> Lincoln Park & Cutty Sark...
> Collard greens & limousines—

Mother *Lila B. Teer* sat like Buddha on an East St. Louis street named Tudor & mentored everybody from Miles Davis to Ike Turner, the Hudlin Brothers to Jackie Joyner, Ambassador Donald McHenry to Joseph Harrison, Raymond Campbell to poet Darlene Roy. Until her death she was a cultural orchestra leader, harmonizing races & religions, rich & poor, youths & adults, urban & rural—all from her post as liaison between SIUE & the City of East St. Louis.

Everyone collects—& gets collected by—people & things. Hence, we're Compilations—of all we've encountered. Perhaps you'll find among these SIUE Ancestors a person or event you'd like to "collect." Perhaps you'll be able to say to your forebears & heirs, as I'm fond of whispering to SIUE, "I Can Never Unlove Thee."

More Than Serendipity?

by ERNEST L. SCHUSKY

When I graduated from Miami University, Ohio, in 1952, I had a major in sociology and only two courses in anthropology. When graduate school beckoned, my major suggested continuing in sociology, while my passion called for anthropology. Unable to decide, I applied to two schools that offered sociology and two that offered anthropology. A scholarship in anthropology decided my future, one that I have enjoyed and would recommend to anyone.

After I finished graduate course work at the University of Chicago, my mentor learned that the University of South Dakota needed an anthropologist to determine why the Lower Brule Sioux Reservation sought "Termination," a Federal policy meant to end U.S. government relations with the Indian tribes. The apparent answer was that the Lower Brule would terminate if awarded one million dollars, in addition to a million dollar settlement for land lost to the newly built Fort Randall Dam on the Missouri River; however, since other reservations experienced similar situations, a fuller explanation required a thorough examination of Lower Brule political organization.

At Chicago there was a working hypothesis that Native Americans appeared incapable of governing themselves because the federal government had held responsibility for all their property; therefore, the Bureau of Indian Affairs (BIA) had assumed authority for economic decisions.

As an example, in the first tribal council meetings I recorded, the tribe made major land purchases and sales involving thousands of dollars. It looked to me as if I were about to disprove the hypothesis; however, it took only a few inquires to learn that the BIA had previously planned which lands should be acquired for ranching and which lands were unfit for ranching. The BIA decided the important issues while the tribal council merely confirmed them. My fieldwork was at a standstill.

When I learned that a small Sioux Episcopal Church intended to host the Annual Convocation the year I lived there, I expected to watch the Sioux fail at this endeavor, not because the BIA had responsibility, but because the congregation had taken on a far too ambitious task. A congregation of fifty families intended to feed five hundred people three meals a day for three days, provide them with safe drinking water and a camping area, build a meeting place for everyone including a platform equipped with a sound system, and maintain law and order. I judged as disastrous the selection of the man selected to be in charge of 'law and order'. He was an ex-convict and the only person I met whom I feared. As an observer-participant, I helped paint the church, but evaded further responsibility so I could not be blamed for what I foresaw as certain failure.

The day after the Convocation ended I sat dumbfounded as I recorded final results. The 'incapable' Native Americans had done everything they had planned—and more. A committee had talked the BIA into resurfacing the road into the reservation, and the bureau had built a bridge over a dangerous stream. Not a single incident of disorderly conduct had occurred under the 'law and order' chair.

I had strong evidence that Native-American communities were perfectly capable of handling their own affairs, and I owed it to a Convocation that came to Lower Brule only once every ten years, and at a time when I just happened to be there.

Serendipity struck again soon after. I had been "adopted" by a family of five brothers, three of them living on the reservation. They helped me with my fieldwork. The youngest brother, who attended South Dakota State University, informed me that the Rural Sociology Department wanted an anthropologist with training in sociology. I applied and, after being accepted as an instructor, I gained experience in teaching and continued my research among the Sioux for an additional two years. I was limited to teaching only introductory anthropology and struggled to prepare additional sociology courses; however, when I went back to Chicago in 1960 to defend my dissertation, I heard about a new campus of Southern Illinois University being built at Edwardsville (SIUE), that intended to hire an anthropologist. Once again, I happened to be in the right place at the right time.

During my first four years at SIUE, while I labored to prepare new courses in anthropology, I recruited a fellow Chicago student as our second anthropologist. The two of us offered classes at Alton and E. St. Louis, while we added new courses in archaeology and cultural anthropology. We faced new preparations each year while planning a major in anthropology.

In addition, since the university encouraged research, I set out to determine differences between patrilineal and matrilineal kinship systems. I prepared a manual illustrating the systems for my student assistants. When a publisher's representative saw it, he encouraged me to submit it to his editor, Holt, Rinehart and Winston. This publisher was preparing a series on methods of research and decided to include my manual in their project. It sold more copies than most in the series, went into a second edition, and was translated into Portuguese. If the *Manual for Kinship Analysis* had not been lying on my desk when the representative visited, the work would never have been published.

Also in my early years, I served as a consultant for the Presbyterian Board of Missions. One project called for a monograph, *The Right to Be Indian,* intended for Presbyterian Women study groups. While on a Post-Doctoral study at the London School of Economics, the Indian Historian Press republished the monograph. With their readership, I reached a wide number of Native Americans and received what I like to think of as my first fan mail. I learned later that professors teaching courses on Native Americans often assigned my monograph.

While SIUE rewarded my publishing, my interests remained focused on the classroom. The second anthropologist, Patrick Culbert, and I assigned what we considered classic works in the introductory course, but we found it necessary to describe basic concepts in handouts. With aid from the university, we produced a printed copy of a short, basic textbook. When a publisher's representative showed interest in it, we submitted it to Prentice Hall. *Introducing Culture* went through four editions and sold over 100,000 copies. It was translated into Korean and Japanese.

In the heady years when children of baby boomers swelled the newly built campus at Edwardsville, enrollments in anthropology reached their height. One quarter I taught two sections of Introductory Anthropology with 237 students in each section, plus a Physical Anthropology class of 48. I believe I may have set a record in Anthropology for number of students taught in a single quarter.

New faculty increased our ranks. A third anthropologist, Fred Voget recruited from the University of Toronto, specialized in theory, and allowed us to offer a major in anthropology. Of course, other departments added faculty along with service units. At Lovejoy Library I met Mary Sue Dilliard, who helped me with historical research on Lower Brule. We soon married and we continue to share research and writing experiences. One result was the production of a history of the Lower Brule Sioux Reservation published as *The Forgotten Sioux.*

Growth at the university accelerated and faculty joked that SIUE was a good place to be away from because coming back was like

Schusky, 2010, returns to anthropology laboratory at SIUE he helped create.
PHOTOGRAPH BY JULIE HOLT.

arriving at a new university. Mary Sue and I went to the Carbondale Campus a year after our marriage. I taught graduate courses in the Anthropology Department while she worked as a Reference Librarian in Morris Library. We may have the distinction of being the only Visiting Professors at our own university.

A few years later, with the aid of a sabbatical, we attended classes in the fall at the University of Arizona, where I gathered data for a book, *Culture and Agriculture*. In the spring, a Fulbright Professorship sent us to South Korea where I taught at Seoul National University. I was amazed at the changes that had occurred in Seoul and in the countryside since I had been there in the Army. Another surprise was a Korean anthropologist with an interest in North

Korean agriculture who helped me add more data for my book. We planned a trip to Japan that summer and found a study group going to China (only study groups were admitted to China at the time). Serendipity struck again. We were able to travel two weeks in Japan followed by three weeks in China.

Near the end of our careers at SIUE, a student from Carbondale—then a professor at the University of Alaska—invited me to Fairbanks to teach for a semester. Mary Sue volunteered in the library. We lived in a historic log cabin with a gigantic fireplace (but also a furnace). Inuit students may have taught me as much as I taught them. Most important, major changes in the relationship between natives and the U.S. government were occurring, and I observed them first-hand.

Now in retirement more than fifteen years, I swim and play tennis to keep active, and study Spanish to exercise my mind. My interest in Native Americans has led me to write historical novels with a goal of educating the public on Indians. *Journey to the Sun* is set in the empire of the Mississippians. It aims to describe the urban life at Cahokia Mounds a thousand years ago. *Ride the Whirlwind* is the adventure of a young man caught in the Pueblo Revolt of 1680. The few Spanish not killed in the countryside fled to Santa Fe. A siege ended in surrender of the Spanish and their exodus to old Mexico. Pueblo Indians kept Nuevo Mexico independent and free from the Spanish for twelve years. In *Return to Beauty,* I portray the capture of a young Navajo, her escape from slavery, and her journey through a dangerous countryside to her homeland in Canyon de Chelly. The book shows the extent of Navajo and Ute slavery on the Spanish frontier and the importance of Indian labor to the Neuvo Mexico economy. *Too Many Miracles* has a contemporary setting in the mountains of Sonora, Mexico. Detribalized Yaquis and Mayos took over their religion when Jesuit missionaries were expelled more than three hundred years ago. Sonoran religion became a blending of Catholicism with native beliefs plus innovation. The mixture resulted in tragedy with comedic aspects. Presently, I am writing about the Tohono O'odham resistance to the 1941 draft to illustrate how

Indians have clung to their way of life in face of massive pressure to behave like whites.

As I look back on my experience at SIUE as a professor of anthropology, I realize that being in the right place at the right time helped my career, but also I needed to heed my passion and to work hard in order to take advantage of the serendipity. Had I not entered intense discussions about Indian policy at Chicago, I would have been unprepared to understand the importance of the Lower Brule Convocation. In addition, countless hours in the library reading U.S government policy toward Native Americans helped me write *The Right to be Indian*. As I look back on my career at Southern Illinois University Edwardsville, I realize that even more important than serendipity is the oft-quoted prescription for success—perseverance and perspiration.

For Further Reading

Those interested in reading more about Cultural Anthropology may wish to visit McGraw Hill's Online Learning Center, an excellent web resource which can be found from most search engines using the keywords: CULTURAL ANTHROPOLOGY | CAREER OPPORTUNITIES or by going to: http://highered.mcgraw-hill.com/sites/0072500506/. This resource covers archaeology and physical anthropology as well as cultural anthropology, and has been posted by Conrad P. Kottak, of the University of Michigan.

January 25, 2011

John D. Kendall Dies at 93; *Leader in Music Training*

by MARGALIT FOX

JOHN D. KENDALL, who half a century ago helped revitalize string playing in the United States by introducing Americans to the Suzuki method, a system of instruction that lets very young children learn to play instruments before they can even read music, died on Jan. 6 in Ann Arbor, Mich. He was 93.

John Kendall
PHOTOGRAPH BY CHRISTY NEVIUS.

The cause was complications of a recent stroke, his daughter, Nancy Foster, said. At his death, Mr. Kendall was emeritus professor of music at Southern Illinois University, Edwardsville, where he had taught from 1963 to 1994, and lived in Ann Arbor.

Developed in Japan after World War II by the violinist Shinichi Suzuki, the Suzuki method lets children begin studying an instrument years earlier than was previously thought possible; it has since been extended from the violin to viola, cello, flute, harp and piano.

Today, at least a quarter-million children worldwide are receiving Suzuki instruction, according to the Suzuki Association of the Americas.

Mr. Kendall was not the only early convert to Suzuki here, but he was by all accounts its most tireless evangelist. In 1959 he spent months in Japan observing Mr. Suzuki's methods firsthand, one of the first Western teachers to do so. He was the first, starting in the early 1960s, to adapt Mr. Suzuki's instructional books for American students; he helped found the Suzuki Association in 1972 and was later its president.

Until shortly before his death Mr. Kendall lectured on the method; conducted master classes around the world; taught private students of all ages; and trained generations of Suzuki teachers.

At midcentury, American string playing was in a precarious state. In a collective anxiety that mirrored the nation's cold-war concern over falling behind in the sciences, music educators bemoaned the fate of the symphony orchestra and in particular its string section.

"In the '60s, string education wasn't doing too well in the United States," Tanya L. Carey, a cellist and longtime Suzuki educator based in Illinois, said in an interview. "Orchestras were hiring foreign musicians, because we weren't producing enough American-trained musicians."

The problem was rooted in American string pedagogy. Children typically began instruction fairly late, at about 10. The curriculum stressed endless scales, arpeggios and other soul-numbing exercises, for most children a deep disincentive to practice.

By contrast, the Suzuki method teaches children as young as 2 or 3. It entails immersion in musical life (classical music is to be played constantly in the child's home); miniature instruments built to fit tiny hands; the learning of real pieces by ear through imitation, with music-reading taught only later; and the intensive involvement of parents, who are trained along with the child and oversee practice at home.

"You don't just drop your kids off and then pick them up," Ms. Carey explained. "There's a triangle of the child and the parent and teacher, and they all work together."

The method is not intended to turn out world-class soloists—although it has, and a good many of them. Instead it aims to produce collegial human beings for whom music is the stuff of everyday life, while discouraging the intense competition that has beset much traditional instruction.

As Mr. Kendall recounted in a privately published memoir, "Recollections of a Peripatetic Pedagogue," this point was driven home to him soon after he returned from Japan. He was lecturing about the method at the Interlochen Center for the Arts in Interlochen, Mich., a hotbed of musical intensity.

"I made the fatal blunder of referring negatively to 'competition,' which, according to Suzuki, has been at the root of humans' troubles throughout history," he wrote. "I was not invited back for 15 years."

John Dryden Kendall was born on Aug. 30, 1917, in Kearney, Neb., and reared on his parents' farm. He began violin lessons as a boy, receiving a bachelor's degree from the Oberlin College Conservatory in 1939; he later earned a master's degree from Columbia University Teachers College.

Mr. Kendall, who was from a Quaker background, was a conscientious objector in World War II. For a time during the war he worked as a mental-hospital orderly on Welfare Island, as Roosevelt Island in New York City was then known; he also served as a subject in an experiment to determine the optimal diet for high-altitude fighter pilots, which involved consuming copious quantities of fat.

After the war, Mr. Kendall joined the faculty of Muskingum College, now Muskingum University, in New Concord, Ohio. In 1958, he attended a music-educators' conference at which he saw a film of 750

Kendall instructs a young girl on violin.
PHOTOGRAPH COURTESY OF PHOTOGRAPHIC SERVICES COLLECTION, UNIVERSITY ARCHIVES, LOVEJOY LIBRARY.

Japanese children playing the Bach Concerto for Two Violins—collectively, spiritedly and very much in tune.

Mr. Kendall was impressed, but his natural inquisitiveness was also aroused. It seemed inconceivable that young children could play complex music so well. Could the film, he wondered, have been rigged?

Seeking an answer, he secured an invitation from Mr. Suzuki, found grant money and flew to Japan the next year, a voyage of 18 hours by prop plane. Arriving in Yokohama, he was met by 250 small children bearing small violins, who flung themselves, in perfect unison, into Vivaldi's G minor Violin Concerto.

"It brought tears to my eyes," Mr. Kendall wrote, "and a feeling that after this experience nothing in the music world was going to be exactly the same."

In 1964, Mr. Kendall helped organize a United States concert tour by 10 of Mr. Suzuki's students. The tour took in 19 cities, including New York; wherever it went, it dazzled parents, educators and news reporters and helped the method gain a foothold in this country.

Today, home-grown Suzuki-trained players are legion in major American orchestras. Many renowned American soloists are also products of the method, including the violinist Rachel Barton Pine, the cellist Wendy Warner and the pianist Orion Weiss.

Mr. Kendall's wife, the former Catherine Wolff, a violist whom he married in 1942, died in 1998. In addition to his daughter, Mrs. Foster, he is survived by two sons, Stephen, and Christopher, who is a lutenist and the dean of the University of Michigan School of Music, Theater and Dance; seven grandchildren, among them the principal violist of the National Symphony Orchestra, the assistant principal cellist of the Philadelphia Orchestra, and the internationally known violin soloist Nicolas Kendall; and four great-grandchildren, ranging in age from 5 to 9, all of whom have their musical education well under way.

FROM THE NEW YORK TIMES ON THE WEB (C) THE NEW YORK TIMES COMPANY.
REPRINTED WITH PERMISSION.

REFLECTIONS ON JOHN KENDALL

by LINDA PERRY

On July 17, 2011, a celebration of the life of John Kendall was held at the Wildey Theatre in Edwardsville, Illinois. These excerpts are from that gathering.

John Kendall was a unique individual who contributed immeasurably to SIUE, to the Edwardsville community, and to the world of music. I was privileged to know him as a colleague at SIUE, as the teacher of my son, as an international leader of the Suzuki movement, and as a remarkable human being who left his mark on everything he touched. Today I would like to share with you some recollections I have solicited from former students and colleagues.

Lloyd Blakely, the visionary first Music Department Chair at SIUE, invited John to teach here in 1963, when the university operated from Alton at the old Shurtleff College and from East St. Louis, two years before the Edwardsville campus opened, Money was apparently not an issue at that time, and Dr. Blakely was told to "seek the best faculty who would come to the new campus and build a quality program from 'scratch'." To start a string program in an area devoid of high school orchestras, he was looking for a strong musician and teacher who could build an area string program in addition to recruiting and forming a resident faculty string quartet. Already a pioneer in bringing Shinichi Suzuki's approach to violin teaching to this country, John accepted the challenge to "write his own ticket" in a brand-new program on a brand-new campus.

John accomplished Lloyd Blakely's objectives in a three-pronged attack. First, he started area children on violin lessons at the Alton campus, using the Suzuki philosophy. In 1965, with the opening of the Edwardsville campus, his first graduate students in Suzuki pedagogy began to come here, starting a long train of 139 students who eventually came to SIUE from throughout the U.S. and 16 countries until John left Edwardsville in 1992. Usually there were about a dozen students each year, and they interned as teaching assistants in the String Development program. This ongoing pre-college program, now 48 years old, currently enrolls 260 area students.

Next, the Edwardsville Public Schools string program was a direct result of John's Suzuki success at SIUE. Enthusiastic parents of the Edwardsville Suzuki students crusaded for years to get a program into the Edwardsville District, and it was finally begun in 1974 with fourth graders only and a half-time teacher. Each year another grade was added, and within nine years there was a 4-12 program in all the schools. By that time there were two full-time string teachers, and there was an outstanding high school orchestra. Now, 37 years later, that legacy remains in the community.

Another element of John's work in the area involved the Lincoln String Quartet, which not only played concerts on campus, but also gave numerous Young Audiences concerts to promote interest in classical music among school children. John was the first conductor of the SIUE orchestra, which presented its "Corridor Concerts" in the hallway of the Peck Classroom Building in the early years before construction of the Communications Building (now known as Dunham Hall).

The need for adequate facilities was a challenge throughout John's tenure at SIUE. Attempts to house the growing string program in the new classroom buildings were less than successful, and John sought refuge in an abandoned and condemned farm house on campus, complete with skunks, snakes, and a leaking roof. It was there that Sven Sjögren, the first of a steady stream of sixteen Swedish students, met John for the first time. When he arrived at the decrepit String House, he could not find Mr. Kendall. He expected a professor sitting in a nice studio, but all he could see was a man in a blue jumpsuit working on the roof. Sven called to him, asking if he knew where the professor was, but of course it was Professor Kendall who was trying to mend the leaking roof.

That old house was eventually demolished, and a slightly more desirable house with no skunks was found on the north edge of the campus. It accommodated the program until John retired, but John continued to repair the roof and other structural problems throughout all those years. The homey atmosphere of the house was integral to the familial closeness the students and the families of the String Development Program felt for one another. This was where, every Thursday morning, John and all the graduate students would congregate around the oval table in a large, attic-style room, first for a master class in which they received instruction on their solo music, followed by a teachers' meeting in which they would discuss strategies for dealing with their young students.

Here are the thoughts of some of John's students. Sylvia Khoo, a delightful student who came from Malaysia in the 80s and is now an outstanding teacher in Singapore, reports:

> Mr. Kendall did not only choose talented, clever or musical students to teach. If he had, I wouldn't have had a chance to study from Mr. Kendall and be a teacher myself today. I might have ended up being a hairdresser or a noodle seller. I was actually a self-taught violin student, as my first teacher in Malaysia was a Catholic missionary priest who never played the violin but was interested in teaching the violin. Mr. Kendall took up the challenge and taught me from scratch "how not to scratch."
>
> Mr. and Mrs. Kendall cared for me and many local and foreign students when they felt that we might be lonely and missed home. I was quite often invited to their home for healthy homemade soup and food. Mrs. Kendall's soup looked so natural and organic that I was quite afraid to taste it. I remember even asking her if she got the ingredients from her moldy pond. With her great sense of humor, she giggled and asked me to try it. After trying it, I wanted more.

Ingrid Johannsen, who came from Sweden in the 70s and now plays in a professional orchestra in Göteborg, relates:

> Everyone knows about Mr Kendall's excellence as violin teacher. But he wasn't just teaching violin. Just as important to me was his interest in helping to form me as a human being, starting ideas and thoughts, and being there as a listener when I needed to talk and ventilate problems. The open home of John and Kay meant a lot, I think especially to us foreign students—their soup and sandwich evenings, Friday coffee with Kay, chamber music sessions, doing pottery, walking around the pond.
>
> To me John and Kay Kendall were real world citizens, who lived their lives according to ideas and principles that we all could benefit so much from.

The children of our area Suzuki families were so fortunate to grow up in this environment. As a testimonial to John's teaching, eight members of John's first international Suzuki Tour Group that traveled to Iceland and Sweden in 1983, now scattered from coast to coast, returned to play a tribute to their revered Mr. Kendall.

The primary goal of the Suzuki philosophy of teaching violin is the enrichment of lives, not training of professional musicians. Only four of the thirteen original group members now play or teach violin as a career, while five are in the medical field, and others include a computer engineer, a special education teacher, a lawyer, and an architect. It is obvious that music still plays a vital part in all their lives, and John Kendall was proud of all their accomplishments.

John was a mentor but also a friend who left behind much more than music education to his students and members of this community. Every time I go to the national Suzuki Association conferences, I see at least 20 former graduate students from around the U.S. and the world, and I realize how far his influence has radiated in all directions from this small city of Edwardsville, where we were all privileged to be at the center of this wonderful movement.

Journey to SUCCESS

by RANCE THOMAS

After my second reenlistment in the United States Air Force, I made the decision that I would retire early enough to start a new career after retirement. Therefore, I began taking college courses in the evenings at the various bases where I was stationed. Before entering the Air Force, I had already attended one year of college and, during my career, I earned enough college credits to be awarded a BA in General Studies. My goal upon retirement was to continue my education and eventually become a director of some social agency that would provide assistance to those with special needs.

Upon retiring at Scott Air Force Base in Illinois, I entered the MA program in Sociology at SIUE, and my schooling and time at SIUE became a transformational period in my life. Not only did my goals change, but my philosophy on life changed as well. This happened because I met a professor, Dr. Robert Lauer, who became my advisor, mentor, and the friend who convinced me to go into higher education. I reluctantly followed his advice because he was such an outstanding teacher and author, and that was very persuasive to me. He not only was my advisor, but he became my friend, and I wanted to emulate him. Although, I did not become a published author, teaching became the most rewarding experience of my life. I am still reaping the benefits of having chosen this profession.

My entry into the MA in Sociology at SIUE was not uneventful. In fact, I entered the program with a great deal of anxiety, because I felt that I might not be able to do the work necessary to earn a degree. These feelings were made even worse by one experience during my first semester in a survey class in sociology. There were approximately 45 students working on their MA degrees in this class and, on the first day, the professor announced to the class that it would not be easy and that approximately half the class would fail. He felt that his class was a class that weeded out those students who were not capable of succeeding at the graduate level.

On the first exam, over half the class failed, and before very long the class had dwindled to approximately 22 students, in part due to students having withdrawn from the class. Even though I had a successful career in the Air Force where I received many awards and had done exceptionally well during my schooling, this situation created even more anxiety within me; however, I remained in the class and, along with many other students, finished it with the grade of "C." The grade shocked me a bit, because I had done above average work previously, except for my freshman year when I entered college several weeks before my 17th birthday. When I graduated from high school at 16 years of age, I did not take college seriously. My father insisted that I take pre-medical classes, because he wanted me to become a physician, but medicine was not one of my major fields of interest; therefore, I just went through the motions of being a college student. Some of the courses in the pre-med program did not interest me. In addition, I could not stand the sight of blood and the thought of having to work with bleeding patients was not very appealing to me.

In contrast, when I had taken evening classes during my service career, I had consistently been on the Dean's List. So, I continued with my classes at SIUE, and in spite of this one experience, I did quite well. I learned that despite the first few weeks in a course that is seemingly difficult, after a while it often becomes easier and more understandable.

My confidence was further enhanced by my research for my thesis. The topic of my thesis was "A Comparative Analysis of Social Change and Stress—England and the United States." This research required that I develop a questionnaire to measure social change and stress in England and the United States. Therefore, I spent five weeks in England administering this survey to students at Oxford University. This was a type of homecoming, because I had spent nine years in England while serving in the U.S. Air Force, and my wife was English. As a result, I had my family with me and spent a great deal of my spare time living with and visiting my wife's relatives during our stay.

At this same time, my advisor was conducting a parallel survey of students at SIUE. We analyzed both surveys, compared data and concluded that social change does indeed cause stress, regardless of whether it is desirable or voluntary. What causes stress is the unknown involved in change. As might be expected, change causes more stress when it is involuntary or undesirable, and we found that it created more stress for English students than for American students, perhaps because the English students were more linked to tradition than the American students. In any case, this was an interesting experience and one that required me to approach individuals that I would not have done otherwise.

Through the survey, I learned to deal with many different types of individuals, some who were friendly and some who were not. Since many English university students are international students, many of these students return to their native countries during the summer. Therefore, I had to go to hundreds of homes in my efforts to find English university students. This made it more difficult because I had to deal with all kinds of individuals, including parents and siblings of students. Some invited me in for tea and cookies and some slammed the door in my face. One homeowner asked me why I was conducting a survey in England, and she told me, "We don't need you Yanks to do our research, we can do our own." Needless to say, this was very unsettling. Fortunately, this was near the end of my surveying. I am really glad that it did not happen at the beginning, because I was very reticent to approach individuals in their homes or at the University in the first place. On the whole, I became used to the process and enjoyed the experience, especially after I had finished it. Nevertheless, no matter what response I received, I continued my surveying because it was necessary to earn my degree.

After this experience, I gained a great deal more confidence that I would be able to do the work at this level, and as I mentioned above, I had a wonderful advisor and mentor who provided support and helped me gain more confidence. In addition, I became a teacher's assistant and worked closely with several other faculty members and their classes. Later, I became the one student member of the Admission and Teachers Assistantship Program for Sociology. Then I became Vice-President of the Sociology's Student Association. Combined, these connections and relationships gave me a better appreciation of the University, faculty, and students. As a result, although the 18 months that it took me to earn my Master's Degree were stressful, they became an enjoyable and meaningful time in my life and very important to my future career in academia and education.

Upon graduation from SIUE with an MA Degree, I accepted a teaching position as an instructor in Sociology and Criminal Justice at Lewis & Clark Community College (LCCC) in Godfrey, Illinois. After working as a professor at the College and co-authoring several journal articles with my mentor, Professor Lauer, I wrote a number of editorial articles in the *St. Louis Post-Dispatch* and *The Telegraph* newspaper in Alton. I was also invited to become a board member of SIUE's Alumni Association. During my ten years on the Board of Directors, I served in various leadership roles, including President during my last two years. By the time I was elected President, I had gained the respect of members of the Board. As a result, to allow me to serve two years instead of one year, the Board changed bylaws that had been in effect since the Association was organized.

As President, I had certain responsibilities that I had not had before. For example, I was a non-voting member of the SIUE Foundation Board automatically during those years, so I was expected to attend Foundation Board meetings. Also as President, I was required to participate in four commencement ceremonies each year, and had to make remarks and present awards during two ceremonies to the Distinguished Alumni of the year along with SIUE teacher of the year during the ceremonies. Needless to say, this was an honor but caused me a great deal of anxiety. In spite of the anxiety, this experience was very helpful, since my later career included speaking engagements at various events within the Metropolitan region.

During my teaching years, I had many wonderful experiences, especially after my third year. I began as an instructor and through the years advanced through the ranks to become a full professor. However, this was not an easy climb. During my first two or three years, it was very difficult. I was an African-American in a college where many students were white and came from rural areas within the college district. Students came not only from Madison County, but they came from the more rural counties of Calhoun, Jersey, Greene, Macoupin, Monroe, etc., where many of them had never seen or had any personal contact with a live African-American. Some told me that they had only had contact with them by watching television or movies. Some also told me that they had never been to St. Louis out of fear of crime and violence; therefore, they had a stereotypical view of African-Americans.

Since a major part of sociology consists of ethnic and race relations, the study of families, various group behavior, etc., racial stereotypes made it even more difficult and was complicated also by the fact that my criminal justice classes consisted primarily of law enforcement officers from local police departments as well as state policemen and sheriff deputies from these same counties. In some of my classes, almost all were law enforcement officers who held similar views as other students from these areas. As part of my courses, I was required to teach about race relations, human relations, deviant behavior and various group behaviors. As one might imagine, it took a great deal of effort and patience to overcome the biases that many had of me and African-Americans in general; however, after a couple of years and a great deal of hard work, I became successful and gained the respect of most of my students and colleagues. Some even became friends and are still are friends today.

I often encounter former students as I travel throughout the community in the Alton area and in North St. Louis County. I recall a recent experience when, within a few weeks period of time, I met six former students, who came up to me and said, "Dr. Thomas, you were my teacher twenty-five or thirty years ago, and I really enjoyed your class" or "You made a difference in my life." These included a teacher, a police chief, a small businessman, several nurses, etc. I had long forgotten some of them, but they recognized me. These are the residual rewards of being an educator. We do not always receive immediate feedback or feelings of a job well done until many years later. At times, as we go through our careers, we do not always feel that we are really making a difference. We may even wonder if it is worth it, but moments like those I recently experienced, make me realize that all the time I spent in getting an education and the efforts expended in attempting to teach students the things they need to know to become successful and productive citizens actually did make a difference to some.

Not only did I have to prove myself to my students, but I had to prove myself to my colleagues as well. This was the case, because there were 85 faculty members at LCCC, and I was the third African-American to become a member of the faculty. Only two of us taught academic courses, while the third taught automotive courses. I was able to achieve respect among my colleagues by becoming a member of the Faculty Association and eventually becoming a leader. After some period of time, I was elected president and served for six years.

Rance Thomas with Essay Award Winners at Dr. King Celebration in 2011.
PHOTOGRAPH BY RACHEL GOMEZ.

Prior to this time the term limits were two year terms with a maximum of four years as president; however, the faculty amended the bylaws to enable me to serve an additional two years.

In the meantime, I became involved in working to improve student achievement and was elected as Chair of the Student Achievement Committee. I served in this position for twelve years. This involved working with students who were on academic probation and suspension and helping them to remain in college or gain readmission by creating opportunities for them to gain the skills or knowledge they needed.

After my term ended as chair of this committee, I did research on minorities' low retention rates and mentoring programs, then I organized a Minority Mentoring Program at the College in an attempt to help minority students adjust to college life and succeed academically. I coordinated this program for ten years. This was important, because when this program began, out of a total student population of 6,000–7,000 students, the College had fewer than four hundred African-Americans students. Many of them were not successful in remaining in college; therefore, the dropout rate was very high. Through this program we were successful in attracting more African-American students and increasing their retention rate. What made the program so successful was the participation of many staff and faculty including the Academic Dean, chairs of various divisions, directors of various departments, faculty, etc. In fact, each of them became mentors and worked with several students a semester in an attempt to help students succeed. This program was unique because the vast majority of mentors were white.

During my whole career, I never lost my desire to work to improve conditions within the community. As a result, I was involved in a number of community organizations that were working to improve conditions. I never gave up the desire to make a difference, and my education and experience often gave me some insight into problems and ways to deal with them. Without my education, I would have not have known how to work with others to make changes within the community. Because of my educational background, I had an opportunity to write publicly on various issues within the community. During my educational training, I had a difficult time writing articles or papers required in various courses; however, because I had to write these papers and take subjects and develop themes around them while in college, I eventually became proficient at it. Of course, it was difficult to overcome initial feelings of lack of expertise, but the more I wrote the easier it became. Eventually, I began to enjoy it. During my career at LCCC, I wrote articles for the editorial pages of the *St. Louis Post-Dispatch* and *The Telegraph* newspaper in Alton. Of course, not all of my articles were accepted for publication by the *St. Louis Post-Dispatch*, but for a number of years, I averaged about two articles per year that were published. I was also invited to write a column for *The Telegraph* and have written regularly for this newspaper for approximately 20 years. I began writing a weekly column, but of course this was too much with my full-time teaching and other activities; therefore, I went to every two weeks and eventually went to once a month, which I have been doing now for a number of years.

One of the enjoyable aspects of writing for *The Telegraph* is that I have the opportunity to write about any subject of my choosing. Therefore, I deal with issues that I feel need to be addressed in the community and society, and these include education, race relations, religion, family, community, political process, economic conditions, etc. Four years ago, I was selected to write a religiously-oriented monthly column in the *Suburban Journal of North St. Louis County*, titled "Spreading the Word." This column allows me the freedom to express my thoughts and beliefs concerning religious beliefs. This has been an enjoyable experience also, and I usually receive favorable comments concerning my column, something not always true of the column in *The Telegraph*, where, in addition to the times I receive favorable comments, I also receive critical comments at times as well. Nevertheless, it is an enjoyable experience and I continue to express my views on various issues of import.

Due to my work with students and the community college in various activities, I became the first faculty member in the thirty-two year history of the College to be awarded the Professor Emeritus status upon retirement. In my retirement, I am busier than ever. Some individuals want to play golf, fish, hunt, travel, etc. after retirement. However, my life is so full of activities that I really enjoy that I do not have time to even think about these activities. In fact, several years after my retirement I served as an adjunct faculty at SIUE for one year. Although I enjoyed this challenge, it was really demanding and was very time consuming.

Because of my education and experience, various organizations and individuals are always asking me to become involved and help them in their efforts. Since I still have the desire to work to improve the conditions of those with special or unmet needs, I find it very difficult to say "no." As a result, I serve on boards, committees, and task forces in many organizations, and I did not really realize how many until recently when the United Way of Southwest Illinois wanted to

Thomas giving a speech at NCCU's Annual Covenant Renewal Ceremony.

PHOTOGRAPH BY BARBARA THOMPSON.

do an article on my contributions to the Alton area, and I needed to list them. I was surprised to realize that there are more than 18 of these commitments, including service as president on four of these boards. These organizations are of various kinds, such as an advisory board member of a hospital and a private Catholic high school. Others include organizations dealing with education, religion, social and community development, youth activities, rotary, race relations, social justice, disability awareness, fine arts, charter school, private high school, public school districts, health care and health education, etc. One of my primary and most demanding involvements is in an organization I co-founded in 1998: North County Churches Uniting for Racial Harmony and Justice. I have been president of this organization since its inception. This organization consists of 22 churches of various denominations within North St. Louis County that are working to bring races together to promote understanding between them. This is a major challenge.

Furthermore, because of my education and experience, I have had the honor of serving in various leadership roles within my denomination, the Presbyterian Church. This has been another of those rewarding experiences in my life. The most recent honor was to serve as moderator of the Presbyterian Church USA's Synod of Mid-America two years ago, for a period of one year. The Synod is located in Overland Park, Kansas, and consists of approximately 500 churches in Illinois, Missouri, and Kansas. This commitment involved a great deal of travel, especially to Overland Park.

As might be expected, these organizations and activities really keep me busy; however, since they are those that enable me to use my training and experience in ways that help me satisfy my desire to help those with special needs, I often do not realize how busy I have become. People frequently ask me, "How do you do it and why do I do it?" My involvement in these activities seems so natural that I really enjoy what I am doing, and I do not notice how busy I am. In fact, I have reached the stage in my life now where I must focus on a greater sense of balance in my life.

During a recent interview by a representative of the United Way, I was asked why I volunteer with so many organizations. Although I had to pause momentarily, the answer came easily and without much thought. I told him that I volunteer because I have been blessed with so much, and I feel that I have a responsibility to share with those that are less fortunate.

I learned many years ago that acquiring material goods and continuing to seek them beyond my own needs is not permanently satisfying and does not create lasting happiness. Material things are temporary and in order to create some meaningful sense of happiness and satisfaction, one has to continue to acquire more and more of these things. I believe that happiness and satisfaction come from sharing one's resources with others less fortunate. These include material goods, gifts, knowledge, talents, etc. Wealth does not create lasting happiness and satisfaction, as many wealthy individuals have come to realize. Some notable billionaires have committed themselves to giving away half their fortunes to worthy causes and to those with special needs, for example, Bill Gates, Warren Buffett, Facebook founder, Mark Zuckerman, etc., apparently realizing that the old adage "money does not buy happiness," really is true.

I do not know of any other profession that would have been more rewarding for me. During my career, I occasionally thought about what it would have been like if I had become a director of a social agency; however, in working with many directors of various agencies, I truly appreciate my experiences at SIUE, Lewis & Clark Community College, and various other organizations. Of course, I truly appreciated the relationship I had with my friend and mentor, Professor Robert Lauer, and his influence upon the direction my life and career took.

Because of my work, involvement, and contributions to my field, SIUE, Lewis & Clark Community College, and the community, I have received numerous recognitions and awards in areas ranging from human rights to religion to outstanding educational achievement. Nevertheless, one of the honors that I am most proud of is that of having been inducted into SIUE Alumni Hall of Fame in the College of Arts and Science several years ago for my commitment to SIUE, my field, and the community.

For Further Reading

Brill, Naomi L. (1973), *Working With People, The Helping Process*. Lippincott Company, Philadelphia, New York, Toronto.

Carnegie, Dale (1990), *How to Win Friends and Influence People*. Simon & Schuster.

Dungy, Tony with Nathan Whitaker (2007), *Quiet Strength, The Principles, Practices, and Priorities of a Winning Life*. Tyndale House Publishers, Inc. Carol Steam. IL.

Maggio, Rosalie (1990), *How to Say It*. Prentice Hall Business & Professional Division, A Division of Simon & SchusterEnglewood Cliffs, NJ 07632.

Osteen, Joel (2004), *Your Best Life Now*. Warner Faith. New York, Boston, Nashville.

Peale, Norman Vincent (1996), *The Power of Positive Thinking*. Galantine Books, Reissued Edition.

Singelton, Glenn E. and Curtis Linton (2006), *Courageous Conversations About Race*. Crown Press, A Sage Publishing Co.

Warren, Rick (2002), *The Purpose Driven Life*. Zondervan, Grand Rapids, MI. 09530.

The Long and Winding Road

by GONZALO JOSE JOVE CUSICANQUI

My journey began in the mid 1960s when my parents decided to leave Bolivia and go to the United States, where they could explore its wonders and provide more opportunities for my siblings and me. We had studied at the most prestigious school in Bolivia—The American Cooperative School—and we had the added privilege of being tutored by two English women. In hindsight, all this education was preparing us to get out of Bolivia.

Bolivia was a poor, underdeveloped country in the 1960s, with no sense of national pride. Going to the United States was everyone's dream, but it was nearly impossible to obtain a visa. When we had briefly visited in 1958 with tourist visas, my parents became enamored with the idea of living there, and my father set up an account with Chase Manhattan Bank of New York. That, together with the solid assets my parents had in Bolivia and the good school grades my sister and I received, would later prove conducive to securing visas for all of us.

In August 1965, our relatives bade us farewell at the La Paz airport. Our destination was Minneapolis, Minnesota, but the two-propeller airplane first made stops in Peru, Colombia, and Florida. From Miami, we took a greyhound bus north to Minnesota. As if the trek wasn't difficult enough for our family of five, only my sister and I spoke English.

It was an uncle on my father's side who lived in Minnesota who received us several days later. He and his family, who we did not know, were kind and helped us find our way. They served as our anchor. We rented a large two-story house on a small hill and attended Holy Name Catholic School for the school year. The parish and neighbors welcomed us warmly and even brought over some furniture and tools—snow shovels and such—things that were vital for surviving the winter. What impressed us was the sense of community and warmth we were shown. All this helped us establish roots in the United States. It was a magical time with many wonderful and fond memories.

In Bolivia, my father had been an accountant and my mother a nurse; however, because the language barrier prevented them from continuing their professions, they now took other jobs. The harsh weather took its toll on my mother; she became ill and had to have gall bladder surgery. Her slow recovery prompted my parents' decision to return to Bolivia, though none of us really wanted to go back. We loved where we were and what we had.

My father, once again with foresight, had purchased a unique vehicle at the time: a Ford Galaxy 500 with more bells and whistles than the twin-engine plane that had brought us to the U.S. It was smooth, comfortable, with push buttons everywhere, automatic this and that, and an AM radio that could pick up stations in Spanish. So we packed our nice ride with as much of the U.S. as we could and headed back south with sadness in our hearts. Our car journey ended in Louisiana, the port of New Orleans where the gleaming white Ford would be shipped and find it's new home in La Paz.

We stayed in La Paz only for a short time before returning to New Orleans, but my father struggled to find work, and our savings were kept in a Savings and Loan Company that went bankrupt. Adding to this situation, a fourth sibling, Angelo, came along. Living in a small, cramped apartment, we waited for funds to be sent from Bolivia so that we could make our next move. My parents had enrolled us in a Catholic Middle School, but even though we had good times in New Orleans, and enjoyed Mardi Gras as well, it was time once again to regroup.

We returned to Bolivia—somewhat tired but not totally defeated —and we stayed for a year, all the while longing for the United States. When we planned our return to the States, we picked St. Louis, Missouri, just because it was located geographically in the middle of the country. It turned out to be a good choice. My dad quickly found a job at Chrysler Corporation, my mom found a job as a nurses' aid, and the children attended St. Francis De Sales.

It was during my time at St Francis de Sales that I blossomed and became very active in all kinds of endeavors. I discovered I had a knack for art and also sports, mainly soccer and wrestling. I was selected to the league all-star soccer team three out of the four years and made MVP wrestler my senior year. I was also involved in student government.

My parents had a path set for my sister and me, which was for us to become doctors. Although that profession did not appeal to us, we felt obliged to pursue it because of the efforts our parents had put forth for us. As soon as we graduated from high school, they enrolled us in the pre-med program at the University of Missouri in St. Louis (UMSL). It was a tough first year for me at UMSL because I still wanted to participate in sports and other activities. Studying was not a big priority. I was still living at home, and my parents were strict with me. I suggested that my sister and I go away to school and my parents reluctantly agreed to send us to the University of Missouri in Columbia—known as Mizzou—to continue with the pre-med program. We lived in dorms and experienced a whole new world and lifestyle. I joined intramural soccer, took a part-time job as a waiter and really enjoyed my stay there. Unfortunately, on the academic front, things were not good. I was simply not interested in medicine, and because my heart was not in my studies, it was not working out.

After a year at Mizzou, my sister and I went back home a bit confused. We knew that we had to study in order to survive in this world, so for our third year, we once again enrolled at UMSL and continued with the pre-med program more out of guilt than anything else. It was crazy, the very definition of insanity: doing the same thing and expecting different results.

Even when things again did not work out at UMSL, my parents did not lose hope and sought out a new place of higher learning. It was 1975, and they were adamant about our success. Southern Illinois University Edwardsville became the place where this would happen. We decided to follow different educational paths, ones that we would enjoy. We found SIUE much more receptive to our weary minds. I enrolled in the Fine Arts Program, despite being worried how about to present this decision to my parents, who had always dreamed I'd become a doctor.

SIUE had a wider variety of subjects and the campus itself was more beautiful. I enrolled in a couple of basic art courses with math always tagging along, by this time calculus. Although I toyed with art in high school, it was here where my passion really began. I thoroughly enjoyed my classes and felt as though a whole new world opened up for me, both in my perception of it and what I was creating with it.

At UMSL and Mizzou, my philosophical views of life had sprouted. The lives people were leading seemed bizarre to me. I did not want to become a robot, did not want to belong to what I perceived as a corrupt system that was being manipulated for the good of a few. After taking the required classes in college, even my outlook on religion changed. I saw religion as a farce, a crutch that people used and a main instrument in helping control a decadent society. I saw money as a necessary evil that made us lose the concept of living as true human beings.

A marriage occurred between my new outlook and my passion for art. It made me happy to be alive and to realize how wonderful the world is in a very pure sense. I saw my life as open and full of thrilling possibilities. Now I would have to sell my father on it, so he could accept me for who I was. He didn't though, no matter how much I tried to explain myself. The result was I had to pay for my own schooling from that moment on.

Nevertheless, life had to go on and art turned out to be my refuge. SIUE provided this refuge for me. I would leave my house at 7:30 a.m., go to classes at the main campus and then retreat to the Warner complex where I would get lost in the wonderful world of art. I had great professors who would encourage my growth, in particular David Huntley and Tom Gipe. Tom was my sculpture professor who was very instrumental in guiding me to major in sculpture. He helped me visualize art in three dimensions, and the iron pours he directed were fantastic. Tom also advised me on where I should go after I graduated. My idea was to attend Washington University School of Architecture, but he vehemently advised me against it, fearing it would curtail my imagination. David Huntley was head of the Art department at the time. He had a vision of artists as great communicators, and this inspired me day after day. He always had time for his students, even though at times he was very direct, almost brutal, in his critiques. Today I understand his honesty, and am glad for it because it helped my growth.

Another very influential person was Philip Hampton, my painting professor. He had a knack for improving my paintings by adding subtle nuances. Years later, I ran into him at the St. Louis Arts Guild, an organization of St. Louis Artists, and he persuaded me to join and exhibit some of my works. I had quite a few shows there and won some awards as well. I really appreciated the ratio of students to professors at SIUE, which I feel allowed teachers like Philip Hampton to remember me and guide me later on in life.

My professors always gave me all the necessary attention. The classrooms and studio spaces were large enough for us to get lost in our work. The art history courses were excellent, and our professor was always looking to build our knowledge by staying extra time to explain, or by giving us more information on a particular artist. That is where my love for art books started. I also remember with fondness the countless field trips where we would go out and draw directly from nature. I would later regularly do this on my own.

My dreamy days had to end at 4pm when I went to work at UPS in Earth City, which was a 45-minute drive from campus. I used that time to eat and reflect on the day and all I was learning. I usually arrived home at 10 or 10:30pm, went to my room, got lost in my art books, drew or played with wax for new sculptures. Those three years flew by and the time came when I had to face reality. I had to figure out what I was going to do with an art degree, something which I was proud of but which the world seemed to have little use for. I had a few projects here and there: designing T-shirts and figures for trophies, also working with cypress wood, designing tables and clocks. Some friends and I would take these on the road to arts and crafts fairs, along with paintings that I had done. The life of a traveling artist was fine since I lived at home and made enough money to buy my supplies, and allowed me to avoid my disapproving father.

Eventually I met my first wife and could no longer live in my fantasy world. It was time to move out of the house, find an apartment and think not only of myself but also of my wife, Astrid. I tried living as an artist but it was not panning out. I had a few shows in small venues and a couple of commissions but the pressures to be a serious provider were too much. I felt the need to look for conventional work and a steady paycheck. Fortunately, my extensive studies in math help me land a job at an insurance firm. As an assistant underwriter, I performed my job at an acceptable level, but had issues with wearing ties and suits. Furthermore, I stayed up late working on my art, which caused me to be unpunctual at work the following day. After several warnings I got fired. I had lasted over a year in the world I detested, was unemployed for a while, and Astrid held down the fort. I tried to earn money through my art, but it was never consistent; I felt pressure to be the breadwinner, which came from my wife, her family, and my parents.

Having to earn money and be responsible, I joined the rat race that I'd always wanted to avoid. My SIUE degree helped me land a management training opportunity at Kenny Shoe Corporation with decent pay. I worked long and hard hours, saw little of Astrid, but always found time for my art and the shows that continued to come my way. I lasted at Kenny's for about a year before the Payless Corporation recruited me for better opportunities and more pay. I got promoted quickly, got shipped out to Chicago to run my own store and was chosen to rewrite the company manual. Although this was quite an honor, I realized that I was getting sucked into a world I was never fond of. I felt somewhat like a hypocrite, but the money was good and, more importantly, it kept my wife and relatives pleased. During my time in Chicago, my art was put on the shelf because I just had no time; it was all work, and I became entrenched in the fast-paced corporate life.

A newer company, Shoe Carnival, recruited and seduced me with more money and greater opportunities. I was sent to Indianapolis. During this time Astrid wanted to start a family and my dream of becoming a full-time artist went again to the very back burner. We stayed in Indianapolis for two years and my two children, Alex and Elena, were born. My job was very demanding because, besides running my store, I was also responsible for overseeing other stores. I received several awards and was considered the "wonder boy" of the company. Gradually we became homesick for St. Louis, so I requested a transfer, which was granted. Things ran more smoothly, and the pressure to move up to the next level was there, but I just continued and even found more time to devote to my art at the expense of ignoring my family, which meant my marriage was suffering. By this time I had accomplished economic goals for my family and was ready for a change. I consulted with Astrid and told her that I did not want to continue the life we were living and that it was time to quit my job, sell the house and do something different. She didn't agree, and this turned out to be the beginning of the end. We got divorced and I left in my truck with some clothes and a bit of cash. I surrendered all my other possessions including the house to Astrid and my kids, and continued to provide for them.

I had turned 40 and was going through a midlife crisis. I was confused and felt like a failure. To top it all off, I received full disapproval from my father not only because I would not let go of my art, but also because of my divorce. The Latino culture places much value on the family, considers it sacred and frowns at divorce. I thought long and hard on how to gain some approval from my father and wanted to show him that I was not completely worthless, so I proceeded to start a business in Bolivia with my two brothers, Angelo and Paul. We opened up a bar that turned out to be a bad idea because we got caught up in too much partying. I was able to produce some art and design work, but overall this six-month stint left me somewhat dry. Fortunately or not, Shoe Carnival urged me to return, enticing me with more money. My obligations and responsibility as a father were thoughts that never left my mind so I promptly returned to the "rat race" but this time with a stronger determination to continue with my art. I was sent to Kansas City and worked there for three months, then was transferred to Macon, Georgia, for an even shorter stay, and finally sent to Orlando, Florida, to a location that was to be the powerhouse of the south for Shoe Carnival. I lived in Orlando for about two years, grew the store into a prime tourist attraction, traveled to Brazil and Argentina, established ties with tour companies, set record store sales and continued to receive awards.

All this happened as my children were growing up, and being far away from them made me feel guilty for not being a good father. I once again requested a transfer back to St. Louis to allow me to be closer to my children. My priorities were my children Alex and Elena, then my art, and lastly my job. The art I produced gave me opportunities to participate in group exhibitions around the St. Louis area as well as in a couple of galleries in Tampa, Florida; more importantly, my art was starting to get noticed. I was invited to have a solo show in the St. Louis Sieberg Gallery as well as to participate in a group show in the New York Agora gallery which was to represent me. Artmine.com was also interested in representing me, so it seemed like I was going in the right direction with my passion and I was excited.

As fate would have it, I fell in love again and married Katie, a young woman full of life. Everything I had set up fell completely apart; she wanted to start a family and once again, my art was going to be the sacrificial lamb. We thought that moving out of St. Louis would help us start a new life, so once again I asked for a transfer. My company needed new blood in the Chicago market so off we went to Gurnee Mills in the outskirts of Chicago. It seemed like a rerun from my first marriage; my daughter Madeline was born and once again I was working long hours, again restarting my new store, overlooking other stores and opening up new ones. I was rewarded well with good pay and additional awards. My time was completely tied up with my new family and my demanding job. This did not last long as I was starting to get anxious and frustrated because once again I fell into the "rat race" trap and could not forgive myself. Katie was much younger than I and needed more attention than I could give her, so this relationship was doomed to fail. It only lasted three years.

After this second divorce, I was far from my children, feeling sorry for myself and turning to alcohol to relieve my sorrow and grief; but, at the same time I was creating some art. I met a wonderful Russian woman Julija, who was also an artist and designer. We fell in love, got married and it seemed like I finally met someone with my same outlook; however, things again fell apart and that marriage only lasted a year and a half.

After yet another failed relationship, I decided it was time to fall in love with my only true love, and that was art. My company needed me back in the heart of Chicago to revive another store and it was perfect for me because I wanted to be closer to the art scene. I rented a large apartment to accommodate my own studio and started to create lots of art, build a foundation for shows, and sold a few pieces. It seemed that a second chance to become what I wanted was coming to fruition. Things were going great but I needed to separate myself from this dual existence. I was starting to get burned out and needed to get away from the Shoe Carnival.

This is when I became aware of a summons for a mural proposal

'Usurpación'— Size: 2.8 meters x 13 meters.
PHOTOGRAPH BY ANDRÉS JORDAN.

in Bolivia and I thought, "Why not?" The subject matter was the struggle of social movements in Bolivian history so I had a lot of reading to do since I had never studied the history of my country. While learning about my roots, the emotional process made quite an impact on me. I could finally communicate in the way David Huntley said we were to do as artists. I cried while painting the first sketches of this proposal because I could feel the pain, struggle and suffering my ancestors had gone through. This piece of art called "La Usurpación del Boliviano" (The Usurpation of the Bolivian) was going to change my life. I sent the finished painting to La Paz and it appeared in the newspapers. This was a good omen that showed me it was time to return home.

By this time my two younger brothers, Angelo and Paul, had been living in Bolivia for years and did not want to return to the U.S. It was through their encouragement that all five of us gathered in my apartment on December 2004 and decided that it was time for all of us to return home as a family to give back all we had learned in the U. S. We all agreed that each one of us had something to contribute, from me as an artist, my sister Elvia as a mass communicator, librarian and animal activist (MA from SIUE, MLS from USF) to my younger brother Paul as a musician (BA from SIUE). Angelo and Charles, my other siblings were also a part of this meeting but their function would be more as support. The plan took two years to get off the ground.

Meanwhile, I still had to deal with my dual existence of working and creating art. I was invited to be in some group shows and one of the galleries that represented me was High Risk Gallery where I had a show that was a mild success and resulted in the sale of a couple of pieces. I sold a few more pieces in Chicago but the pressure from Shoe Carnival to help out in other stores frustrated me and though I felt like quitting, I knew I had to endure another year.

Perhaps my employers at Shoe Carnival could read my ambivalence; they beat me to the punch by letting me go, in part because they were going thru a restructuring phase (and knew that I had no interest in pursuing anything new with them), but probably also because I was earning a very good salary, but was no longer committed to the company.

'La Evolución de La Ley'– Size: 2.66 meters x 7.23 meters.
PHOTOGRAPH BY ADRIAN VERA.

I left Chicago to start a whole new phase in my life and was so excited that finally after all the trials and tribulations, my time had come. Though it was long overdue, I had no one else to blame but myself and had no regrets. It was time to head back home to St. Louis, regroup my thoughts and goals and look forward to the best part of my life. I stayed in St. Louis for about six months, shedding my corporate skin and going through therapy by remodeling and painting murals in my parents' house. Meanwhile I was invited to participate in a group show at Bellas Artes Gallery and also taught some courses at The St. Louis Art Museum. They offered me a job as a resident artist, but I had to turn it down since my life was planned out in Bolivia.

At the same time, my brother Paul opened up a Vegetarian Restaurant in La Paz. Once I got there, we expanded and created an alternative space, which would include an art gallery. I immediately started painting every wall that was available, decorated the restaurant with murals and sculpted walls with Gaudi as my guide. His innovative designs had always inspired me even while attending SIUE.

'Organic Movements'— Various dimensions.
PHOTOGRAPH BY ADRIAN VERA.

I was ready to contribute to the world as an artist and explored the art scene by visiting the main art school "Academia de Bellas Artes" to look for students who wanted to show their work in our new gallery. During this process, I was able to recruit three artists who would be very instrumental in endeavors over the next three years.

During this time in Bolivia, Evo Morales became the first indigenous president. My country is going through major social and structural changes as well as through a cultural revolution. The majority of Bolivians are indigenous and now they have a voice and are determining their own future. The small minority who were running the country since the mid 1800's finally were ousted from power. This is a very special time in the history of the world because another oppressed minority is claiming its right in the sun. This feeling of change is in the air; the racism that was so prevalent in years past is being addressed but those roots run very deep and it will take generations for it to subside.

Parallel to this non-violent revolution, we painted a mural in the center of town, a reproduction of the painting I had done in Chicago "Usurpación del Boliviano." It was the opportune time to paint this mural. It was well received by the general public, the government and mass media. Through foreign press interviews, my mural reached the international community. A close up of it is on the cover of the college textbook "Surrendering To Utopia" by Mark Goodale, which is an anthropology of human rights. This recognition prompted us to paint more murals throughout La Paz; furthermore, I was commissioned to paint a piece for a professor at the University of Bremen, Germany, that portrays South America as the "Hope" for the world. I was also asked to lead a group of students from around the country to paint a mural and a sculpture for our president. We even had breakfast with him at the "Palacio De Gobierno," our version of the White House.

Today we are a busy group of artists with Vidal Cussi, Sofia Chipana and Ramiro Acarapi, being the main drive of this artistic endeavor. Presently we are working on two projects simultaneously;

a mural depicting the revolutionary fight of the university students from a world wide prospective. This sad and bloody story has to be told so that future generations can reflect and understand where their liberties came from. We are also working on our first sculptural project, a statue of the Goddess Themes, better known as the Lady Justice.

By the way, we are receiving support from our Vegetarian Restaurant, who we call our Pacha Mama (Mother Earth), because she has and is taking care of us throughout this whole time. Her name is, "Namaste," and every day she brings us all sorts of people from all over the world who enjoy our food, our art, our music and all the things we present as true human beings who care for all living things. Life is a gift; if you hold on to your dreams and give it all your love and devotion, and never give up on yourself, you can make things happen.

Unique Opportunities in HIGHER Education: Some Thoughts from a Retired Sociology Professor

by JOHN E. FARLEY

The roots of my interest in sociology undoubtedly go back to my childhood experiences. Television brought live to my middle-class Iowa living room the struggles of the Civil Rights movement in the South during the late 1950s and early 1960s. The images of police beating and fire-hosing young children, who asked only to be treated the same as other children with a different skin color, haunted me then and in many ways still do. A more personal impact of this country's racial turmoil reached me on a hot summer day after I graduated from high school, as I lay in bed with an untimely case of the mumps. This time the television networks were showing pictures of my hometown, Waterloo, Iowa. The night before, America's nationwide urban upheaval of the "long, hot summer" of 1967 had reached even there, as crowds battled police, broke windows, looted, and threw firebombs. A lot of people in my town professed no understanding of what was going on. I thought about a classmate of mine—white like me—who had complained about a carload of African Americans driving through his neighborhood. "Don't they understand that they can never live here?" he had asked. It seemed to me there might be some connection between that attitude and the violence that was occurring across town.

Although my decision to study sociology came later, I think its seed had been sown by then. And there is no doubt that this seed greatly influenced what I did in my career as a sociologist in higher education, a career that provided unique opportunities to address the kinds of problems that brought me to this career in the first place. Much of my research throughout my career in higher education focused on housing segregation along racial lines, and I taught courses on race and ethnic relations nearly every semester at Southern Illinois University Edwardsville. My first book was a textbook on race and ethnic relations, now in its sixth edition (Farley, 2010). I found that I enjoyed writing textbooks; they were a great way to turn others on to the excitement I found in sociology, so I went on to write more, including one on social problems and an introduction to sociology. The introductory sociology book is entering its sixth edition, and now has a coauthor who is a former student of mine from the master's program in sociology at SIUE. That student went on to get a Ph.D. and is now a professor at Daytona State College in Florida.

By about a decade into my career as an academic sociologist, I had become frustrated that my exposés on housing segregation in the St. Louis area had not led people to do more about the problem. Using data from the 1970, 1980, and 1990 U.S. censuses, I had documented that the St. Louis metropolitan area was one of the most racially segregated areas in the country, and that segregation was a pattern that extended across all parts of the metropolitan area-city and suburbs, Missouri and Illinois. Moreover, my research also clearly showed that segregation was not simply a matter of where whites and African Americans could afford to live. Rather, white and black residents of the St. Louis metropolitan area remained extremely separated from each other within all income groups. Poor whites

In 1998, Dr. Farley served as President of the Illinois Sociological Association and brought the Association's Annual Meeting to East St. Louis. One session, shown here, was held jointly with the Eugene Redmond Writer's Club's annual Break Word With the World event.

PHOTOGRAPH BY EUGENE REDMOND.

lived apart from poor African Americans, middle-class whites lived apart from middle class African Americans, and wealthy whites lived apart from wealthy African Americans. Race, not income, accounted for segregation in the St. Louis area. I thought that by exposing the extent of segregation in the St. Louis area and documenting that it was tied to race, not class, I could enhance public awareness of the problem of racial segregation and discrimination in housing, and that, as a result, people would take action to do something about it. This, it turns out, was naïve.

It was at this time that I fully realized the importance of *applying* sociology—using sociological techniques to attack social problems. Working with a small group of other concerned citizens, I formed the Metropolitan St. Louis Equal Housing Opportunity Council (EHOC), an organization using the sociological technique of the fair housing test to uncover housing discrimination. Using this technique, two people of different races visit apartment rental or real estate offices seeking housing in order to see if they are treated the same or differently. We found widespread discrimination and took action against it. In one case, a cooperative effort with the U.S. Department of Justice found three apartment complexes in St. Louis County that were refusing to rent to African Americans. This discrimination finding resulted in a settlement costing one of the apartment complexes $30,000. Tests in another part of St. Louis County found that whites seeking to buy houses were sent to one side of a major thoroughfare, while black home seekers were nearly always sent to the other side—an illegal practice called *racial steering*. These tests, too, led to a costly settlement paid by one of the real estate agencies involved. As a result of EHOC's efforts, we believe today that housing providers who might be inclined to discriminate are thinking twice about discrimination, because they now know they could get caught, and if they do, there will be consequences.

In addition to creating the opportunity to actually *do* something about the problems of housing discrimination and segregation in the St. Louis area, forming EHOC was also rewarding because of the opportunities it offered for my students. A number of SIUE students, both undergraduate and graduate, became involved in the fair housing movement in various ways. Dozens of SIUE students over the years have served as discrimination testers—the people who visit housing providers to see whether home-seekers of different races, genders, disability statuses, family statuses, and sexual orientations are treated the same, as federal, state, and local fair housing laws require[1], or whether illegal discrimination occurs. Students who have served in this way have gained invaluable experience in learning how to carry out a valid, unbiased test, accurately record and report results, and other skills relevant to conducting accurate research.

---

[1] Federal fair housing law forbids discrimination in the sale, rental, financing, and insurance of housing on the basis of race, color, religion, national origin, sex, disability status, or familial status (i.e. discrimination against families or households with children). Illinois law and St. Louis city ordinance also forbid housing discrimination on the basis of sexual orientation.

In so doing, they also have the reward of knowing that they have helped to prevent unfair and illegal discrimination in the sale and rental of housing.

A number of students have also performed internships at EHOC. Some years ago, the sociology department at SIUE became a leader in making changes in its programs to make a sociology degree more relevant to students' gaining employment opportunities after graduation. It did this by establishing an applied-sociology specialization in employment relations within the undergraduate sociology curriculum, and the addition of internship options for students in both the undergraduate and graduate sociology programs. Internships offer students the opportunity to use what they have learned in the classroom in an on-the-job situation, and at the same time gain valuable experience in a real workplace situation. A number of undergraduate and graduate students at SIUE have completed internships at EHOC over the years. A few have gone on after graduation to work at EHOC on a part-time or full-time basis.

Finally, EHOC has brought valuable experiences to students in the classroom at SIUE. In my race relations classes as well as in my urban sociology summer workshop class, I invited EHOC staff to make presentations about housing discrimination in the St. Louis area and what was being done about it. This brought my students into contact with the realities of discrimination and with efforts to address it in a way that purely academic course material never could have. Thus, for all these reasons, I found that my involvement with EHOC not only offered me a way to get something actually done about the problems my research had revealed, but also offered a wide variety of valuable opportunities for my students.

As I look back at my 30-year career as a sociology professor (29 of those years at SIUE) and my preparation for that career as a graduate student at the University of Michigan, I feel fortunate to have had a career that allowed me to do what I loved to do—conduct social research and offer students an opportunity to see what could be learned through the social sciences and how the social sciences could be used

Professor Farley delivers his presidential address to the 2001 meeting of the Midwest Sociological Society, held in St. Louis.

PHOTOGRAPH BY RANDY REYNOLDS.

to improve people's lives. I also realize that in higher education, you have unique opportunities to influence people's lives for the better—and you don't always know when and where those opportunities will come along. I would like to finish my chapter with an example that I hope will be relevant to any students reading this chapter, and one that shows that the opportunities higher education offers for betterment of the world are there for students as well as for faculty members.

Most of what I have discussed so far addresses opportunities to make people's lives better that I was able to utilize as a college professor. I now realize that one of my biggest opportunities came along while I was still in graduate school, although I did not fully realize it at the time. While I was a graduate student at the University of Michigan, an effort was undertaken to unionize the university's graduate teaching and research assistants. I became involved in that effort, because it seemed to me that it was important to recognize that graduate assistants were performing valuable work for the university—teaching large numbers of students and doing much of the day-to-day work of research at the university. Yet, the compensation they received at the time did not reflect the value of the work being done. At that time, only one other such union existed in the United States, at the University of Wisconsin. During the course of our union's negotiations with the university, a major issue that arose was our union's request for a clause banning discrimination on the basis of sexual orientation. No union had ever asked for that before at the University of Michigan, and at the time, that was considered a radical idea.

After prolonged and contentious negotiations, our union eventually came to agreement with the university and we gained what was just the second graduate-assistant union contract in the United States. Among the items in that contract was a ban on discrimination on the basis of sexual orientation. At the time, we had no way of knowing what lasting accomplishments these would be. Both graduate-assistant unionization and protection against discrimination based on sexual orientation are ideas that have become widely-accepted today. The union we formed still represents graduate assistants at Michigan 35 years later. Today, there are more than 30 universities in the United States with recognized bargaining agent unions for graduate assistants, including all of the University of California system and about half of the Big Ten universities. There are more than 20 more such unions in Canada. So what we at Michigan and some fellow graduate students at Wisconsin began in the 1970s has now become widely-institutionalized today.

Similarly, only a few years later every union at the University of Michigan had a clause banning discrimination on the basis of sexual orientation. Protection against this type of discrimination has become the law today in most states. About twenty states ban discrimination on the basis of sexual orientation in all employment, and ten more ban it in state employment. And even in states without laws against such discrimination, there are many cities that do have such laws and union contracts and corporate policies that forbid it. So what seemed like a new and radical idea when our union proposed it has today become a widely-accepted right. It is rewarding to know that I was able to play some part in that, and in the recognition of the basic employment rights of graduate assistants.

So the common feature in what I have recounted in this chapter is that higher education offers tremendous opportunities to help create a better world. Such opportunities exist for faculty members, both in the new worlds of learning that they can offer to their students and in the research they carry out and the opportunities that exist to act on that research to create a better world. They also exist for students through various options and activities available on every major campus, and as in my experience with the graduate assistant union, you may not realize at the time what potential for long lasting change for the better may lie in those opportunities. Of course, the other common feature is that you have to take advantage of those opportunities. EHOC was not going to form on its own just because my research and that of others showed that housing segregation and discrimination are major problems in the St. Louis area. Similarly, recognition of the workplace rights of graduate assistants and of the wrongness of discrimination based on sexual orientation was not going to happen unless somebody did some pushing and insisted that these issues be addressed. Part of the message here is that, while such opportunities are always out there, you have to take advantage of them, and at the time you will not have the luxury of knowing what substantial and long-lasting benefits may arise from your action. But my experiences tell me that when you take advantage of the opportunities, the benefits can be great indeed.

For Further Reading

Farley, John E., and Michael Flota. *2011 Sociology, sixth edition.* Boulder, CO: Paradigm Publishers.

Farley, John E. 2010. *Majority-Minority Relations, sixth edition.* Upper Saddle River, NJ: Prentice Hall.

Farley, John E., and Gregory D. Squires. 2005. *"Fences and Neighbors: Segregation in Twenty-First Century America."* Contexts: Understanding People in Their Social Worlds 4, 1: 33-39.

Graduate Employee's Organization. 2011. *"About GEO."* World Wide Web, http://www.umgeo.org/?page_id=3 </P></BOX>

POSTSCRIPT

In Academia as Well, What's Past is Prologue

by ALDEMARO ROMERO

Institutions of higher education in the U.S. are often not very good at recording their own histories. With the exception of a handful of venerable ones, comprehensive narratives about colleges and universities histories are virtually non-existent.

This is somewhat surprising given that, for tenure and other reasons, the workforce which operates in those institutions tends to be rather stable throughout the years. They represent the heart of the institution. The story—probably apocryphal—is told that when Dwight Eisenhower became president of Columbia University in 1948, he was introduced to a lot of distinguished faculty members during his first days in office. When he asked why he was being introduced to those people instead of touring the facilities on campus, the person setting up his agenda told him "because faculty **are** the university."[1]

That story reflects the belief that students and administrators may come and go but faculty, for the most part, stay and do not simply work at a university, but actually constitute it.

---

[1] Although this is a sometimes-repeated story, neither researchers at the Eisenhower Library nor the authoritative *Eisenhower at Columbia* by Travis Jacobs (Transaction Publishers, New Jersey, 2001), provide any substantiation to it.

The idea behind the collections of stories in this current book came after the publication of a previous book, *Adventures in the Academy*[2], a year ago. That volume was a collection written by faculty members of the College of Arts and Sciences (CAS) at Southern Illinois University Edwardsville (SIUE) in which they described their experiences in both the classroom and the field, in the U.S. and abroad. So the next question was logical: how did we get here after more than 50 years of history at SIUE?

Historians know that there is nothing better than primary sources, whether written documents or oral histories, to help us in our attempts to understand past events. The problem with the written record is that many documents in academia tend to be very administrative in nature and are discarded after a certain number of years; however, narrative accounts of previous faculty members may provide a first-hand look into a history that would otherwise be lost.

For this volume, we approached distinguished emeriti faculty and alumni and asked them to share their stories with us. In some cases, those stories needed to be told through an interview, a creative piece, or through writing not by them but about them. The stories of those who graduated from this institution years ago, when this was a smaller and a commuter campus, were also quite compelling. Both narratives together complement each other and give us a wonderful look at memories of teaching and learning in this evolving university.

After reading all those accounts, one comes to the conclusion that this institution has changed a lot during its first fifty years. Its own evolution and success has been the result of the work of dedicated people, but also of adaptation to new ideas, the kind of students we serve, the types of contributions we are making to the community in which we live, and the way internal resources have been managed.

The title of this postscript paraphrases one of Shakespeare's passages in *The Tempest*, but as with many of Shakespeare's phrases,

---

[2] LaFond, L., C. Berger & A. Romero (Eds.). 2010. *Adventures in the Academy: Professors in the Land of Lincoln and Beyond.* Edwardsville: College of Arts and Sciences, SIUE.

the deep meaning and meanings contained within this phrase reach beyond his own time.

We could say that we cannot escape our own past, that some traditions are to be kept, that certain values are never to be modified. Yet, we know that the world is changing quickly and the rate of change is accelerating, not only from a technological viewpoint but also from a cultural one. Examples that directly affect higher education abound: less financial support from state governments, more resistance to increases in tuition and fees in trying to remedy budgetary shortfalls, changes in attitudes and preparation among students coming from high schools, higher levels of diversity in the student body, greater demand for accountability regarding what we do; increasing pressure for higher graduation rates rather than just higher enrollment numbers; the list could go on and on.

So the question is, can we not only survive those challenges but also thrive in new environments, in a world that is more competitive, global, and which holds fewer available resources?

To that end, we need to look at what past generations of university members did to get us where we are today. Although some tactics and approaches must change in different times, certain strategies and practices should not be that different: commitment to excellent, imagination and creativity when confronting new problems, maintaining the sense that we are working not for ourselves but for the public good, and believing that there is no higher reward than to see our students succeed, not simply because of facts they learned while in college, but because of the way we taught them how to think.

If our own history has taught us anything, it is that those individuals who have succeeded have done so not because of simple luck but because of their talents, perseverance, and sheer commitment to being good at what they do. And that is what a liberal arts education is all about: helping individuals, regardless of their background, to discover what their talents are and how to use them best for the benefit of society.

About
THE AUTHORS

RALPH WILLIAM AXTELL was born in Norfolk, Nebraska and spent his early years in Norfolk, Fremont, and then Omaha, Nebraska. After the World War II began, his family moved to Texas, and he graduated from Bishop High School, Bishop, Texas in 1946. Shortly thereafter, he enlisted in the U. S Army and spent 15 months with the U.S. Occupation Forces in Japan. Returning home in 1948, he began studies at the Texas College of Arts and Industries in Kingsville, Texas and later transferred to the University of Texas at Austin, where he received a BA degree in 1953, MA in 1954, and PhD in 1958. In 1960, he joined the SIU Biology Faculty on the old Shurtleff College campus in Alton, Illinois. He served as Biology Faculty Chair from 1965 to 67. After moving to the new Edwardsville campus in 1965, he became General Herpetology Editor for the American Society of Icthyologists and Herpetologists journal COPEIA in 1968 and continued in that position until 1972. He was later elected Fellow of the American Association for the Advancement of Science (AAAS) and President of the Society for the Study of Amphibians and Reptiles (SSAR). He has published approximately 100 illustrations, maps, and peer reviewed papers.

JOHN E. FARLEY is Professor Emeritus of Sociology at Southern Illinois University Edwardsville, where he retired in 2006 after a 30-year college teaching career. He is the author of four books and more than 25 journal articles as well as a number of book chapters and research reports. He has also made numerous presentations on his research at conferences and symposia throughout the United States and at international conferences in Germany, Sweden and Canada. Professor Farley has served as President of the Midwest Sociological Society, the Illinois Sociological Association, the SIUE Faculty Senate and the Metropolitan St. Louis Equal Housing Opportunity Council. His awards and honors include the SIUE Dr. Martin Luther King, Jr. Humanitarian Award; the SIUE Outstanding Scholar Award; the SIUE Kimmel Community Service Award; and research grants from the National Science Foundation and the National Institute of Mental Health. Dr. Farley received his PhD from The University of Michigan and also holds MA degrees in sociology and urban planning from The University of Michigan.

About the Authors

WILLIAM GRIVNA has been a teacher and professional actor/director for over 40 years. He is now Professor Emeritus in the Department of Theater/Dance at SIUE. Bill is a former member of The Guthrie Theatre Company in Minneapolis. On film and television he has appeared as Dulinski, a Polish immigrant, in director Ang Lee's feature film, "Ride with the Devil—the Director's Cut", and in the TV mini-series, "Murder Ordained," as Chappy. Locally, he has been an Associate Director for both Theatre Project Company and HotCity Theatre. When he is not teaching theatre or acting and directing, Bill practices and teaches T'ai Chi, and is also a Life Skills Coach.

GONZALO JOSEPH JOVE was born on August 10, 1955 in La Paz, Bolivia. After traveling back and forth between Bolivia and the United States, Gonzalo and his family settled in St. Louis in 1969. He attended St. Francis De Sales High School and graduated in 1972. From there, he attended University of Missouri St. Louis for two years, continued his college education at the University of Missouri Columbia for one year, and then completed his Bachelors of Fine Arts in Sculpture in 1978 at Southern Illinois University Edwardsville. For 20 years Gonzalo worked in retail management, while exhibiting his artwork across the Midwest, as well as in New York. Gonzalo was also involved in a teaching program with the St. Louis Art Museum. In 2007, Gonzalo made his way back to La Paz and founded San Pedro Studios, which continues to produce murals and inspirational art for the public.

LARRY LAFOND, is Associate Dean of College of Arts and Sciences and Associate Professor of the Department of English Language and Literature at Southern Illinois University Edwardsville. He is a co-editor of this volume and was also co-editor of the predecessor volume, *Adventures in the Academy: Professors in the Land of Lincoln and Beyond*. Elected to Phi Beta Kappa in 2010, Dr. LaFond's academic expertise is in linguistics and his research focuses on second language acquisition, the role of linguistic theory in language teacher education, and regional dialects. He obtained his BA in Biblical Languages from Concordia College, an MA in Applied Linguistics from Old Dominion University, and a PhD in Linguistics from the University of South Carolina. He is co-founder of the Illinois Dialect Project (www.illinoisdialects.com), research that is currently documenting variations in dialect among speakers of English in Southern Illinois.

JOE MUNSHAW came to SIUE in 1972 and retired in 2004. He earned a PhD in Rhetoric and Public Address from the University of Missouri–Columbia in 1972 (elected to Phi Beta Kappa in 1969, and commissioned as a 2nd Lieutenant and Distinguished Military Graduate U.S. Army ROTC in 1971). He won the Central States Speech Association Outstanding Young Teacher Award in 1975, and SIUE Junior Faculty Teaching Excellence Award in 1976. A pioneer in the development of interpersonal communication pedagogy, he developed and taught a wide variety of courses at SIUE, including Interracial Communication, Patterns and Processes of Intrapersonal Communication, Honesty and Deception in Communication Relationships, and Communication Theory. Munshaw's central focus always remained in the classroom. Throughout his career he was a laugher deeply committed to the idea that seriousness is a disease, and that people discover wisdom more readily when smiling. In retirement he lives with his wife, Coke Hennessy, in Manchester, Missouri, and walks life's pathway as an unaffiliated mystic. His grandchildren call him Coyote Joe.

About the Authors

Pianist **LINDA PERRY** is Professor of Music and Director of Keyboard Studies at SIUE. Active in the national Suzuki movement since 1977, and accompanist since 1992 for the national conferences of the Suzuki Association of the Americas, she was invited by their violin committee to collaborate in recording the revised Suzuki Violin repertoire for international distribution. Dr. Perry holds BA and MA degrees in Piano Performance from Northwestern University, and the Doctor of Musical Arts degree in Collaborative Piano from the University of Illinois.

EUGENE B. REDMOND was named Poet Laureate of East St. Louis (Illinois) in 1976, the year Doubleday Publishing Co. released his best *Drumvoices: The Mission of Afro-American Poetry*. Earlier, he spent two years (1967-69) as Teacher-Counselor and Poet-in-Residence at Southern Illinois University's Experiment in Higher Education (East St.Louis) where he taught with Katherine Dunham. From 1970-85, he was Professor of English and Poet-in-Residence in Ethnic Studies at California State University-Sacramento. During that time he won a National Endowment for the Arts Creative Writing Fellowship, an Outstanding Faculty Research Award, a Pushcart Prize: Best of the Small Presses, and served as a visiting professor at universities in the U.S., Africa, and Europe. In 1986, a year after he returned home to East St. Louis, local authors created the Eugene B. Redmond Writers Club in his honor. He rejoined SIUE in 1990 as Professor of English and founding editor of *Drumvoices Revue*. Author/editor of more than 25 volumes of poetry, collections of diverse writings, plays for stage and TV, and the posthumously published works of Henry Dumas (1934-1968), he received an Honorary Doctor of Humane Letters Degree from SIUE in 2008.

WILLIAM RETZLAFF, co-editor for this volume, holds BS (Auburn University), MS (Auburn University) and PhD (Clemson University) degrees in Forestry, with a minor in plant physiology. He has Post-Doctoral experience in Horticulture (Clemson University), Viticulture (UC Davis), and Environmental Sciences (Boyce Thompson Institute for Plant Research). He also managed the commercial vineyards at Six Mile Creek Vineyards for six years while in Ithaca, New York. Dr. Retzlaff has published in a variety of journals in forestry, air pollution, horticulture, green roof, and environmental issue areas. Dr. Retzlaff is internationally recognized for his work on green roof systems and is currently the research co-director of the St. Louis metropolitan area research collaboration (G.R.E.E.N.—Green Roof Environmental Evaluation Network; www.green-siue.com) based at Southern Illinois University Edwardsville.

ALDEMARO ROMERO, co-editor of this volume, is the Dean of the College of Arts and Sciences at Southern Illinois University Edwardsville. He received his bachelor's degree in Biology from the University of Barcelona, Spain, and his PhD in Biology from the University of Miami, Florida. He has published more than 620 pieces of work including books, peer-reviewed articles and articles in non-peer-reviewed publications. His academic interests range from environmental and evolutionary biology to history and philosophy of science and science communication. He has been awarded many grants and has won several awards for teaching and his writing of popular science articles and the writing, production, and direction of both radio and TV shows about science.

ERNEST L. SCHUSKY, born in 1931 in Portsmouth, Ohio, graduated from high school in 1949 and Miami University (Ohio) in 1952. He began graduate work in anthropology at the University of Arizona but service in the Army interrupted his study. With aid from the GI Bill, he finished his PhD at the University of Chicago in 1960. He began his career at the University of South Dakota as a Research Associate, doing field-work at the Lower Brule Sioux Reservation. From 1958 to 1960 he was an Instructor at South Dakota State College. He became Professor of Anthropology at Southern Illinois University Edwardsville in Fall 1960 until his retirement as Professor Emeritus in 1993.

DR. JACK G. SHAHEEN is an internationally acclaimed author, devoted humanist and media critic. He is the recipient of two Fulbright teaching awards [Lebanon and Jordan], and has given over 1,000 lectures in nearly all the 50 states and three continents. Among the many universities that have welcomed him are Amherst, Brown, Emory, and Harvard. World capitols where he has lectured include London, Berlin, Prague, Istanbul, New Delhi, and Cairo. Shaheen is the author of four books: *Nuclear War Films, The TV Arab*, the award-winning book [and DVD-www.relbadarabs.com] *Reel Bad Arabs: How Hollywood Vilifies a People*, and *GUILTY Hollywood's Verdict on Arabs after 9/11*. His writings include 300-plus essays in publications such as *Newsweek, The Wall Street Journal* and *The Washington Post*, to chapters on media stereotypes in dozens of college textbooks. Shaheen, an Oxford research scholar, also served as a CBS News Consultant on Middle East Affairs, and he worked as a professional film consultant with producer Chuck Roven on *Three Kings* (1999), and writer-director Steve Gaghan on *Syriana* (2005).

DAVID SILL, Professor Emeritus, was most recently Senior Scholar and Professor of Design in the Department of Theater and Dance. He joined the faculty in 1980 as a lighting and scene designer and was chair of Theater and Dance from 1987 to 1991. After serving as Acting Dean of the School of Fine Arts and Communications from 1991 to 1995, he was Associate Provost at Southern Illinois University Edwardsville for thirteen years and Acting Provost for two before returning to the faculty. In addition to over 100 design credits, David has published articles on assessment, capstone experiences, continuous quality improvement, and creativity. He is a Peer Reviewer for the Academic Quality Improvement Program where he chairs the AQIP Reaffirmation Panel and serves on the Admissions Panel.

MARIAN SMITH completed her PhD in Botany at the University of Kansas, and taught at SIUE from 1987 until her retirement in 2008. She established a large research program in the Department of Biological Sciences devoted to studying rare and endangered plant species native to the Illinois River Floodplain. She and her students published 42 peer reviewed papers, presented more than 130 papers with published abstracts at regional and national conferences, and published a large number of agency reports. Her research was supported by the National Science Foundation, the US Army Corps of Engineers, the USDA, state conservation agencies in Illinois and Missouri and a variety of private companies. Dr. Smith received the first Paul Simon Award, the first Hoppe Award, and the first Distinguished Professor Award awarded by the Graduate School. She is a member of Sigma Xi, the National Science Honor Society, and was twice selected as the Researcher of the Year by the SIUE Chapter. She is a Fellow of the Illinois State Academy of Sciences and a member of that organization's board. She has recently been awarded the US Fish & Wildlife's highest service award for her work with rare and endangered species.

About the Authors

RANCE THOMAS received his BA in General Studies at the University of Nebraska, in 1968 while serving in the U.S. Air Force. Upon retiring from the Air Force in 1971, he entered Southern Illinois University at Edwardsville's Graduate School where he was awarded an MA in Sociology. In 1985, he was awarded his PhD in Sociology from St. Louis University. In 1973, he had become a faculty member at Lewis & Clark Community College (LCCC), where he retired in 2002. At LCCC, he was Professor of Sociology and Criminal Justice and Coordinator of the Sociology Program. He has been a Columnist for The Telegraph Newspaper in Alton (general topics) for approximately 20 years and has been a Columnist for the Suburban Journal of St. Louis County (religious topics, "Spreading the Word") for approximately four years. Dr. Thomas is an ordained Elder in the Presbyterian Church USA. He is cofounder and President of North County Churches Uniting for Racial Harmony and Justice (22 Churches of various denominations) and serves on numerous Boards, four as president.

SHEILA VOSS serves as the Vice President of Education at the Missouri Botanical Garden, helping guide and strengthen the Garden's mission-driven efforts to engage and inspire current and future generations of local and global citizens. Her team includes passionate educators based at the Garden's main campus, Shaw Nature Reserve, Sophia M. Sachs Butterfly House and Litzsinger Road Ecology Center. Prior to joining the Garden, Sheila served as corporate director of education and conservation for the SeaWorld, Busch Gardens and Discovery Cove parks. Today, Sheila remains a founding Board Member of the non-profit *SeaWorld & Busch Gardens Conservation Fund* and also serves on the Board of Trustees for *Forest ReLeaf of Missouri,* an organization focused on restoring and protecting trees and forests. Sheila holds an MS in Environmental Sciences from Southern Illinois University Edwardsville and a BA in English/Communications from Pennsylvania State University. In her spare time, she strives to spend as much time as possible in the great outdoors– hiking, biking, gardening, exploring and playing. A native Floridian but lover of Midwest seasons, Sheila currently resides in Edwardsville, IL.

JOSEPH A. WEBER received his BS in Art from Eastern Illinois University an MS in Art Education from Indiana University, Bloomington, and a PhD from St. Louis University. He attended the School of the Art Institute in Chicago where he studied graduate painting and art history. He has exhibited paintings in many professional juried exhibitions throughout the Midwest and at exhibitions in Canada and China. His paintings are included in many private and corporate collections in the United States and Canada. After ten years as a teacher of art in Edwardsville, he was hired in 1973 by SIUE to teach art education in the Department of Art and Design. Dr. Weber was president of the Illinois Art Education Association from 1989-1991 and was later recognized by the Association as a Distinguished Member for his contributions and dedication to the field of Art Education. He serves on the City of Edwardsville's Historic Preservation Commission, has been recognized by the Illinois Humanities Council (receiving the Studs Terkel Award), and was recognized in 2008 by The Illinois Association of Historic Preservation Commissions for significant contributions to Historic Preservation in the State of Illinois.

Index

Academie voor Beeldende Vorming, 102
Acarapi, Ramiro, 157
Adventures in the Academy, vii, 168, 174
Agent Orange, 51
Albrecht, Marcus, 82
Albuquerque, xv
Alestle, 23, 106
Alton and East St. Louis Residence Centers, xi
Alton Residence Center, x
Alton, viii, xi, 79, 106, 117, 128, 136, 138, 140, 142, 172, 179
American Association of Higher Education, 86
American Association of State Colleges and Universities, 87
Anderson, Rob, 49
Anheuser-Busch, 16
Arizona State University, xv
Arizona, xiii, xv, 119, 177
Art Institute, 94, 180
Art Therapy, 97-100
Aschenbrenner, Joyce, 110
Axtell, Ralph W., v, xiv, xviii, xix, 172

Badalamenti, Louis, 31
Barber, Samuel, 42-44
Beard, Earl, 78
Beaver Dam Mountains, xv
Beijing, 3-5
Benowitz, William C., 110
Bentley, Kathryn, 8-9
Black Hills, 65-66
Black Power, 51
Black Pride, 51
Black Theater Workshop, 8
Blakely, Lloyd, 128
Blount, Dale, ix, x
Bolero, 41
Bolivia, 145-147, 152, 154, 156-157, 173
Botany, 61-65, 69, 178
Boulder Dam, xv
Boyce, Walter, xiii
Branson, xiii
Broadbooks, Harold, viii
Broughton, xii
Bruce, Betsey, 30
Buffett, Warren, 143
Bureau of Indian Affairs (BIA), 116
Busch Entertainment, 14, 17-18

Cahokia Mounds, 108, 120
California, 17, 22, 33, 73-74, 109
Campbell, Raymond, 110, 113
Canada, 82, 165, 172, 180
Canadian Rockies, 60
Carey, Tanya L., 124-125
Central States Speech Association, 55, 174
China, 1, 3-8, 10, 120, 180
Chipana, Sofia, 157
Cimarron River, xiii
Cohen, Allen, 30
Colbert, Lisa, 8
College of Arts and Sciences (CAS), SIUE, vii, viii, 89, 168, 174, 176
Colorado Plateau Province, xiv
Colorado River, xiv
Colorado, xiii
Columbia University Teachers College, 125
Columbia University, 167
Columbia, 21-22, 147
Congress of Racial Equality, 112
Cornwell, Clifton, 49
Costas, Bob, 30
Cottage Grove Fault, xii
Culbert, Patrick, 118
Cusicanqui, Gonzalo Jose Jove, v, 145
Cussi, Vidal, 157

Davis, Joseph, viii
Daytona State College, 160
Department of Art and Design, 97-98, 180
Department of Biological Sciences, xviii, 178
Department of Speech and Theatre, 48
Department of Theater and Dance, 78, 81, 178
Dilliard, Mary Sue, 118-120
Dixon, Jim, xvi
Duellman, Bill, xvi
Dumas, Henry, 110-111, 175
Duncan, Robert (Bob), 26-27
Dunham, Katherine, 109, 111-112, 175

Eaker, Tom, 31
Early Jurassic Period, xiv
East St. Louis, viii, xi, 26, 79, 105-106, 110-113, 128, 161, 175
Edgecliff College, 74-78, 80, 82-83, 87-88
Edwardsville Earthquake, xi
Edwardsville, Illinois, viii, x, xi, xii, xviii, xix, 10, 19, 25, 31, 47, 66, 68-69, 77, 106, 118, 128-129, 131, 172, 179-180
Eisenhower, Dwight, 167

England, 101, 135-136
Environmental Sciences Program, xviii, 112

Farley, John E., v, 159-161, 164, 172
Feeney, Bill, 83-85
Fine Arts Academy, 94
Florida, 14, 146, 152, 160, 176
Forrester, Lennox, 48
Foster, Nancy, 124, 127
Fox, Margalit, v, 123
France, 33, 101
Freeman, Leonard, 28
Freund Farm, ix, x
Freund, Leopold A., ix, x
Fuller, R. Buckminster, 112

Gates, Bill, 143
General Office Building, 49, 54
Geological Society of America, xii
Germany, 157, 172
Gipe, Tom, 149
Giverny, 101
Glen Canyon Dam, xiii-xiv
Graebe, Annette, 53
Grand Canyon National Park, xiii
Great Basin Collared Lizard, xv
Great Basin Rattlesnake, xv
Gricevich, Max, xiii, xviii
Grivna, William, v, 1, 6, 9, 173

Hampton, Philip, 149
Hardy, Bob, 30
Harrison, Joseph E., 112-113
Hawkins, Robert, 26
Helicopter, viii, ix, xviii, xix
Hornback, Vernon "Ted", 109
Hunter, John, 31
Huntley, David, 26, 149, 154

Illinois, xi, 51, 66, 73, 79, 99, 124, 128, 133, 136, 141, 143, 160, 172, 175, 178
Illinois Board of Higher Education, 79, 86
Illinois Dialect Project, 174
Illinois Education Association, 82-84
Illinois Federation of Teachers, 83
Interracial Communication, 53-54, 174
Iowa, 159

Japan, xi, 106, 120, 124-126, 172
Jason, Emil, 112
Johannsen, Ingrid, 131
Jones III, Taylor, 112
Jones, Chuck "Roadrunner", 29

Kansas, xii, xiii, xv, 62-64, 143
Kansas City, xii, 62, 71, 152
Keevin, Tom, 69
Kendall, John D., v, xviii, 55, 123-131
Kendall, Kay, xviii, 130-131
Kendall, Nicolas, 127
Kennedy, Bobby, 50, 74
Kennedy, John F., 50, 107
Kenny Shoe Corporation, 151
Kerber, Steve, x
Kerr, James, 33
Khoo, Sylvia, 130
King, Jr., Martin Luther, 9, 50, 74, 106, 172
Klobnak, John, 31
Kochan, Robert, 31

LaFond, Larry, ii, vii, 174
Lake Mead, xv
Lauer, Robert, 133, 136, 144,
Lazerson, Earl, viii, 78-81, 83, 85, 88
Lee, Bruce, 10
Lena, John, 27
Lewis & Clark Community College, 136, 144, 179
Library of Congress, 13
Lincoln String Quartet, 129
Litzsinger Road Ecology Center, 18, 179
Long, Leonard, 112
Louvre, 101
Lovejoy Library, ix, 23, 28, 30, 35, 40, 49, 56, 79, 105, 113, 118, 126
Lower Brule Sioux Reservation, 115, 118, 177
Lucatz, Noah, 112

Matta, Michael, 26
Maer, Peter, 30
Malaysia, 130
Markagunt Plateau, xiv
Martin, Craig, 62
Mass Communications, 7, 22-24, 27, 31
Metropolitan St. Louis Equal Housing Opportunity Council (EHOC), 161-163, 166, 172
Mexican Federal District, xvi
Mexican Hat, xiii
Mexico City, xvi
Miami University, 115, 177
Michigan State University, 74
Millett, Richard, 26
Minner, Jack, 31
Minnesota, xix, 146
Mississippi River Festival (MRF), 55-56
Missouri, 21-22, 98-99, 143, 147, 160, 174, 178

Missouri Botanical Garden, 18, 70, 179
Mitchell, Robert, 8
Montane Graphic Lizard, xvii
Monument Valley, xiii
Morris University Center, 49
Morris, Delyte, viii
Mt. Carmel, xiv
Muleshoe Bend, xiii
Munshaw, Joe, v, 47, 174
Muny, 54
Museum of Natural History, x, xii
Muskingum College, 125
Musse d'Orsay, 101
Myer, Donal, viii

National Gallery, 101
National Public Radio (NPR), 24
Native American, 100, 116-118, 120-121
Navajo Sandstone, xiv
Netherlands, 101-102
Nevada, xv
New Mexico, xiv, xv
North Africa, 59
North Carolina State, 61
North Central Association of Schools and Colleges, 86
Nuclear War Films, 26-27, 177

Oberlin College Conservatory, 125
Office for Cultural and Social Diversity, 8
Ohio, 109, 115, 125, 177
Oklahoma, xiii, xv, 59-60
Oregon, 73
Oxford University, 135

Painted Desert, xiii
Paladin, Michael, 31
Paris Philharmonic, 33
Paso de Cortés, xvi
Payless Corporation, 151
Peck, 49-50, 129
Performing Arts Training Center, 109
Perry, Linda, 175
Peru, 146
Pfeifer, Harold, viii
Pine, Rachel Barton, 127
Pitts, Paul, 47
Plaschke, Bill, 27
Pompidou Centre, 101
Popocatepétl (Popo), xvi
Prairie Dogs, xiii
Precambrian Terrain Boundary, xii

Rachmaninoff, Sergei, 38-41
Redmond, Eugene B., v, 105-106, 109, 111, 161, 175
Rendleman, John, viii, 24-25, 54-57, 78
Retzlaff, William A., ii, v, vii, 176
Richmond, Dick, 30
Rider, John, 22, 24, 28
Rijksuseum (Van Gogh Museum), 102
Robertson, Linton, xvi
Romero, Aldemaro, ii, v, vii, 33, 167, 176

Salt Lake City, 60
San Juan River, xiii
San Pedro Studios, 173
School of Dental Medicine (SIU), x
School of Fine Arts, 48, 80, 85, 178
Schusky, Ernest L., v, 115, 119, 177
Science Building, xi, xii, 49, 55, 67
Scotland, 59, 112
SeaWorld, 14, 179
See, Harold W., xi
Senseman, Bob, 27-28
Seoul National University, 119
Shaheen, Jack G., v, 21, 23, 30-31, 177
Shahn, Ben, 94, 96-97
Shanghai Theatre Academy, 3, 5, 7
Shaw Nature Reserve, 18, 179
Shaw, Buzz, viii, 78, 81, 88
Shaw, Will, ix
Shiprock, xiii
Shoe Carnival, 151-153, 155
Shurtleff College, viii, x, 128, 172
Sill, David, v, 8, 73, 75, 84, 178
Simon, Abbey, 42
Sisters of Mercy, 74, 87-88
Sjögren, Sven, 129
Sledge, Ina Peabody, 113
Slenczynska Kerr, Ruth, v, 33-35
Smith, Marian, v, 59, 66-67, 69-70, 178
Smothers, Tommy, 28-29
So, Jacky, 17
Sophia M. Sachs Butterfly House, 18, 179
South America, 59, 157
South Dakota, 65, 115
South Dakota State University, 117
Southern Illinois University, xi, 43, 117
Southern Illinois University Edwardsville, SIUE, v, vii, viii, x, xvi, xviii, xix, xx, 1-2, 7-10, 13, 15-19, 21-22, 24, 27-31, 33, 43, 47-48, 50-58, 66, 68-69, 71, 76-88, 91, 97-103, 105-106, 108, 112-113, 117-118, 120-121, 124, 128-129, 133-137, 141, 144, 148-150, 154, 156, 160, 162-163, 168, 172, 173-180

Southwestern Illinois Campus, xi
Southwestern Illinois University, xi
Southwestern Oklahoma State University, 59
Speech Communication, 47-49, 52-53
Spirituality and Sustainability Center, 49
Springfest, 57-58
St. Louis Art Museum, 27, 156, 173
St. Louis Black Repertory Company, 2
St. Louis Post-Dispatch, 26, 30, 136, 140
St. Louis Repertory Theater, 75
St. Louis Symphony Orchestra, 55
St. Louis, Missouri, 14-15, 18, 21-22, 24, 27, 54, 67, 69, 78, 98, 137, 147, 151-153, 156, 160-163, 166, 173
Steinberg, David, 86
Stringer, Sir Howard, 29
Suburban Journal of North St. Louis County, 141
Suzuki, Suzuki Program, 55, 123-129, 131, 175
Suzuki Association of the Americas, 124, 175
Sweden, 131, 172
Sweezy, C. Otis, 11

Tate and Tate Modern, 101
Teer, Lila B., 113
Teeters, Barbara, 84
Texas, xv, 82, 110, 172
The Telegraph (Alton), 136, 140-141, 179
The American Cooperative School, 145
The Gardens at SIUE, 19
The Nature Preserve Foundation, xviii
The Watershed Nature Center, xviii
Thomas, Rance, v, 133, 139, 179
Tiananmen Square Turmoil, 3, 6
Toscanini, Arturo, 41
Total Cost Assessment (TCA), 17
Traditional Theatre Institute (Beijing), 3
Tudor, William, 27

United Kingdom (UK), 59
United Scenic Artists 829, 82
United States (US), 25, 44, 83, 123-124, 127, 135, 145-147, 164-165, 172-173, 180
United States Institute for Theater Technology, 81
University Assessment Plan, 86
University Center, 49, 55
University Chorale, 55
University of Alaska, 120
University of Arizona, 119, 177
University of California, 73-74, 165
University of Chicago, 115, 177

University of Iowa, xix
University of Kansas, xii, 61, 178
University of Michigan, 127, 163-165, 172
University of Missouri Columbia, 49, 147, 173-174
University of Missouri St. Louis, 147, 173
University of New Mexico, xv
University of South Dakota, 115, 177
University of Toronto, 118
University of Wisconsin, 164
US Army Corps of Engineers, 69, 178
Utah, xiii, xiv, xv

Valley, Dave, 49, 53
Van Camp, Leonard, 26, 55
Vandegrift, Vaughn, viii, xi
Vengerova, Madame Isabelle, 42
Vietnam War, 50
Virgin River Bridge, xv
Voget, Fred, 118
Voss, Shelia, v, 13, 179

Wabash Valley, xii
Walsenburg, xiii
Ward, William, 26-27
Warner, Wendy, 127
Washington Post, 26, 177
Weber, Joseph A., v, 91-92, 180
Webster University, 75
Weiss, Orion, 127
Werner, David, viii, 88
Weyenberg, Tim, xiii
White, Hollis, 48
Wiley, Deane, 27
Wilson, Rudy, 8, 54
Winter, Doralice, 24-25
Winter, Kamil, 24-25
Wolff, Catherine, 127
World War II, 24, 53, 124-125, 172

Xavier University, 75-77, 87

Yunian, Zhang, 5-7, 10

Zion National Park, xiv
Zuckerman, Mark, 143